THE STORY OF INDIAN CIVILISATION

THE STORY OF INDIAN CIVILISATION

C. E. M. JOAD

GYAN

Published by

Gyan Publishing House
5, Ansari Road
Daryaganj, New Delhi-110002
Phone: 011-47034999, 9811692060
E-mail: books@gyanbooks.com

Distribution Network
gyanbooks.com
India, USA, Canada, UK, Australia

ISBN: 978-93-6780-663-0 (PB)

First Published, 1936

2nd Impression 2024

Printed at: Gyan Press, Delhi.

THE STORY OF INDIAN CIVILISATION
Author: C. E. M. JOAD

THE STORY OF INDIAN CIVILISATION

BY

C. E. M. JOAD

AUTHOR OF 'THE STORY OF CIVILISATION, 'COUNTER ATTACK FROM THE EAST,' 'GUIDE TO PHILOSOPHY,' 'GUIDE TO MODERN THOUGHT,' ETC.

MACMILLAN AND CO., LIMITED
ST. MARTIN'S STREET, LONDON
1936

CONTENTS

INTRODUCTION

The following pages were written in response to a suggestion made by an Indian reader of my book, *The Story of Civilisation*, to the effect that the mode of treatment adopted in that book might with advantage be applied to the civilisation of India. *The Story of Civilisation* was written for a series, the *How and Why* series, intended for reasonably intelligent children of from twelve to fourteen years of age, and its length was some 25,000 words. Now it is obvious that, if you set out to tell the story of the achievements of mankind in 25,000 words, you can put in so little, you must leave out so much, that your method will be highly selective. What, then, will determine your selection ? What you think important or significant. Important or significant by what standard ? By the standard of the author who interprets significance, who assigns importance, according to his personal scale of values. Thus the very fact that it is *this* particular selection and not *that* which determines the contents of your book, transforms it from the objective record which it purports to be into the expression of a highly personal point of view. My own selection was such as might be made by a pacifist and an internationalist, convinced that war is the greatest scourge of mankind and believing that only by the gradual establishment of international government can war be ultimately superseded. Accordingly, I left out the battles and the generals, put in the musicians and the thinkers, and emphasised the extent to which man's old-fashioned political organisation lags behind his new-won scientific and economic powers and deprives him of the benefits which they hold in store for him.

The Story of Civilisation appears to have been read scarcely at all by children, but considerably by adults, a circumstance which encouraged me to proceed with the suggestion to give it a successor. For while English children, I am told, read very little, Indian students at the universities read anything and everything they can lay their hands on. In offering them—for it is for them that I have primarily written—this modest sketch of the civilisation of which they are the heirs, I ask them to bear in mind the conditions and circumstances in which it came to be written. I have not attempted to present a complete history, or even a history complete in outline, of India. My plan has been to select those aspects of Indian history which have seemed to me significant or distinctive, and to try to give some account of them, and, as my interest is mainly attracted by the thought and culture of India, these, rather than the political history of the country, have pride of place.

I am in no sense an authority on India. I have never visited the country and have to rely for my view of it upon reading and talk, upon fairly extensive talk, with Indian students visiting England. Thus the book that follows is in the nature less of a scroll continuously unfolding, and revealing as it unfolds, the whole pageant of Indian life and thought, than of a series of historical vignettes. It is like an impressionist sketch that seeks to present a picture of some brightly coloured scene rapidly observed by the artist, and rendered from a highly personal standpoint almost at the moment of vision. The writing of history, I am well aware, must from its very nature be informed by a subjective element. For written history is a record of events seen through the spectacles of Mr. X. Y., a limited and partial personage, living in a particular age, a member of a particular civilisation, the child of a particular environment and the inheritor of a particular culture. Inevitably, then, it throws by implication almost as much light upon the civilisation from within which Mr. X. Y. is recording as upon that which he ostensibly records. Accredited historians make every effort to minimise or at least to disguise this element of the personal and to present as objective a record as in the nature of things is possible. In the present case, however, such efforts have been lacking. I have not tried to disguise personal likes or dislikes, nor have I shrunk from expressing personal opinions. What follows is, therefore, less the story of Indian civilisation, than an account of the reactions produced by that story in a highly interested spectator, a product of the very different civilisation of the West, whose primary purpose in writing has been to make clear to himself what it is that India has or has had which marks off her civilisation from that of all other peoples, and how much of this "something", which romantic writers call "the spirit of India", may be discovered and applied for the benefit of the West. I want to know, too, how much of the enterprise and efficiency of the West India may safely adopt without danger to her "spirit" or to what still remains to her of it.

Such information as this book contains, such authority as it possesses, are due to Girija Mookerjee but for whose collaboration it could not have been written.

C. E. M. JOAD.

HAMPSTEAD,
LONDON, *July* 1936.

OUTLINE OF INDIAN CHRONOLOGY

ANCIENT INDIA (*Circa* 3000 B.C.-A.D. 320)	Earliest hymns of *Rig-Veda*	1200-1000 B.C.
	Upanishads	1000 B.C.
	Rise of Maurya Empire	650 B.C.
	Buddha born	563 B.C.
	Mahabharata	*circa* 400 B.C.
	Alexander's invasion	327 B.C.
	Accession of Asoka	274 B.C.
	Death of Asoka	237 B.C.
HINDU INDIA (A.D. 320-1192)	Rise of Gupta Empire	320
	Samudra Gupta	326-375
	Kalidasa (poet and dramatist)	400-450
	Sankaracharya (philosopher)	789-820
MOSLEM INDIA (A.D. 1192-1757)	Conquest of India by Mohammed Ghazni	1192
	Rizia, Queen of Delhi	1236-1240
	Disintegration of Delhi Empire	1327-1347
	Invasion of Tamurlane	1398, 1399
	Vasco da Gama landed at Calicut	1498
	Mogul dynasty founded	1526
	Akbar	1556-1605
	English Factory established at Surat	1613
	English Trade concession in Bengal	1634

MOSLEM INDIA—(A.D. 1192-1757) *continued*	Death of Aurangzeb -	1707
	Invasion of India by Nadir Shah - -	1738
	Political Revolution in Bengal - - -	1757
BRITISH INDIA -	Battle of Plassey - -	1757
	Rebellion of the Indian Army - - -	1858
	India under the Crown —Royal Proclamation	Nov. 1858
	Indian Councils Act -	1892
	Morley-Minto Reforms -	1909
	Montague-Chelmsford Reforms - - -	1919
	Round Table Conferences - - -	1930-32
	New Constitution - -	1935

CHAPTER I

SKETCH OF INDIAN HISTORY THE MINGLING OF THE RACES

§ 1. Sketch of Indian History

The early history of India is still very imperfectly known. Until recently most historians were disposed to date the beginnings of Indian history at about 1500 B.C., when the first Aryan wanderers from Central Asia came flooding through the passes of Afghanistan and gradually settled down upon the banks of the Indus in North-western India.

Pre-Aryan India, before 1500 B.C.—But recent excavations at Mohenjo Daro in the Indus valley have laid bare the relics of a civilisation, which, according to many scholars, dates back beyond the time of the first Aryan settlement in India. This civilisation bears important resemblances to the Sumerian civilisation in Babylonia, and the view is, accordingly, coming increasingly to be accepted that, long before the Aryans appeared, there existed in India a highly flourishing civilisation exhibiting many features in common with the early civilisations which grew up round the banks of the Euphrates and the Nile Valley. The traces of this earliest Indian civilisation are unfortunately so scanty that its nature is largely a matter of conjecture. Such as they are, however, they do seem to suggest that centuries before the coming of the Aryans human beings living in India were already thinking, reading, writing and creating objects of beauty.

The Aryan Invasions.—It was about 1500 B.C. that the Aryan tribes from Central Asia began to invade India. They came, as the invaders of India have usually come, through the passes on the North-west frontier. With the invasion of the Aryans the records begin to fill out so that for the first time we are able to speak of the history of India. The Aryan invasion was not a single act, but a continuous process. Over a period of hundreds of years wandering Aryan tribes came seeping into India bringing strife and turmoil in their train. Nevertheless, the Aryans were a unifying force, in the sense that they were the first race to impose their personalities upon India as a whole. When the Aryan invasion was over, we can for the first time legitimately speak of "an Indian civilisation"; and this Indian civilisation is predominantly an Aryan civilisation—that is to say, its customs, institutions and religion are all Aryan in origin and character.

Rig-Veda, 1200–1000 B.C.—The earliest record of these peoples is to be found in the books of sacred writing known as the *Rig-Veda*. The *Rig-Veda* which seems to have been composed somewhere between 1200 and 1000 B.C. consists largely of religious hymns and songs of lyrical piety. These hymns and songs are written in Sanskrit, a highly developed language, which is so closely related to Greek and Latin as to render it a plausible conjecture that the

Greek and the Latin peoples sprang from the same ancestors as the Indo-Aryans. Three other Vedas, known as the *Sam*, the *Yaju*, and the *Atharva*, were composed after the *Rig-Veda*. The language of these three later books of sacred writings is different from that of the *Rig-Veda*. They consist of an elaborate series of rules for ritual observances and forms of worship, and are still looked upon by the Hindus as sacred literature.

The Epics, "Ramayana" and "Mahabharata".— The next landmark in India's story is constituted by the two famous epics, the *Ramayana* and the *Mahabharata*. These relate the histories of a number of royal dynasties and give a vivid picture of the condition of the times when they were written. For this reason they are often compared with the Greek epics, the *Iliad* and the *Odyssey*.

The society which they depict consists of a number of independent, highly organised states. For this reason it is thought that they must have been written long after the more primitive Vedas. The weapons described in the epics also show a great advance on those mentioned in the Vedas.

Another set of epics, known as the Puranas, is also extant. These, which were probably composed much later, are chiefly poetical works, partly legendary and partly discursive and controversial in character. They were composed in glorification of special deities. There are eighteen principal Puranas (maha-puranas) and about the same number of secondary Puranas (upa-puranas). The oldest of the Puranas was probably composed in the fourth century A.D.

A more detailed account of the epics will be found in the chapter on *The Search for Expression.*[1]

Origin of Castes.—It was during the period when the Puranas were being composed that Indian society was definitely organised on the lines of the four castes. These were, (1) *Brahmanas*, the priests; (2) *Kshatriyas*, the warriors; (3) *Vaisyas*, the merchants; (4) *Sudras*, the slaves. The caste system is distinctive of and peculiar to Indian civilisation and we must pause here to say a few words about it, although we shall deal with it more fully in the next chapter.[2]

The caste system does not appear to have been instituted until after the Aryan tribes had established themselves in India. There is, for example, a mention of the four castes in only one hymn of the *Rig Veda*. The system was originally devised with the object of dividing the community into groups according to the functions which the members of each group performed in society. There is some evidence that the castes were originally elastic and flexible, so that a man could pass from one to the other; but they subsequently became rigid and fixed, and have remained so up to the present day. The growing rigidity of the castes was largely due to the pressure of social problems. The Aryans were anxious to keep their race pure and to prevent intermarriage with the original inhabitants of the country who were darker in complexion. Consequently the fourth or slave caste, to which the original inhabitants belonged, was officially forbidden to intermarry with

[1] See Chapter IV, pp. 90-92. [2] See Chapter II, pp. 36-42.

the others. At the same time the caste system was designed to give Indian civilisation a certain unity and to prevent the division of the people into hostile factions. It was with the same unifying purpose that the early law-givers, in spite of their own belief in a single God, incorporated into their doctrines many religious ideas of non-Aryan origin, which were polytheistic in character.

General Characteristics of Indian Disposition.—Indian history has been distinguished throughout by a tendency towards toleration. Other peoples' faiths have been preserved, other peoples' customs respected; and not only preserved and respected, but assimilated. Such toleration is a very rare thing in the history of mankind, as rare as it is valuable, and I shall have more to say about it in a later chapter.[1] For the present it is worth while pausing to take note of the fact that the predominant Aryan race, although seeking to preserve its racial purity intact by laws against intermarriage—laws which were not in practice very strictly observed—permitted and encouraged free social intercourse with other races, and even incorporated many of the social and religious institutions of the original inhabitants into the structure of their own society.

This unifying tendency in politics is paralleled by a similar tendency in religion. Faced by a problem, whether of politics or of theology, the typical question which Indians have asked themselves is, how unite many different themes into a single harmony? How, in fact, impose unity on diversity? Thus through-

[1] See Chapter II, pp. 38, 39.

out the whole course of Indian history, the characteristic Indian endeavour has been to look for the common element in apparently different things, the single reality that underlies the apparently many appearances. This endeavour is, as we shall see in the next chapter, the distinguishing feature of Indian religious and philosophical doctrines. It is interesting, then, to note this same insistence upon unity, this same endeavour to unite many into one as exhibited by the early law-givers and administrators of India. At the very beginning of Indian history, we find men trying to reconcile the conflicting ideas held by different people with regard to the right way of living together in society and the right way of conceiving God.

The Maurya Empire.—Until about 650 B.C. there are no records of any Indian dynasty, but in the middle of the seventh century B.C. Bimbisara founded the Maurya Empire. The Maurya Empire constituted the first serious attempt to unify India politically into a single State with a central government.

Buddha.—In 563 B.C. Gautama Buddha was born. It is probable that he was a member of the Sakya tribe, and that his birthplace was Lumbini, near Kapilavastu, the capital of the Sakyan republic. Buddha is the greatest man that India has produced, and one of the two greatest religious teachers that the world has seen.

The Persian Invasion.—About 500 B.C. Darius, the Persian Emperor, sent his admiral, Skylax, to the Indus valley. Skylax sailed down the Indus with his fleet and appears to have annexed both the Punjab and Afghanistan.

Alexander's Invasion, 326 B.C.—Towards the end of the fourth century B.C. Alexander the Great, who had already conquered Persia, marched towards the East, and is believed to have crossed the Indus in February, 326 B.C. In India he met with serious opposition only from Porus, King of Jhelum. Porus was vanquished, and brought in chains before Alexander, who asked him how he would like to be treated. "As a king," was the proud reply. Alexander was impressed with his bearing, and made Porus his viceroy and ally.

300 B.C., *Megasthenes*.—After Alexander's death his successor in the East, Seleucus, invaded India in the year 305 B.C., but was defeated. In the meantime the Maurya Empire founded by Bimbisara had grown powerful under Chandragupta. To Chandragupta, Seleucus sent an ambassador named Megasthenes, who wrote the history of the period. Megasthenes's history introduces us to a highly centralised State with a well-developed administrative system, punishing crime and protecting citizens from violence.

Artha-Shastra.—Another record of the period is to be found in the *Artha-Shastra*, that is, the Manual of Politics, written by Kautilya, also known as Chanakya, who is traditionally reputed to have been Chandragupta's prime minister. The *Artha-Shastra* discusses fully and frankly the arts of government and diplomacy, and shows a well developed sense of political realism—that is to say, it shows how men and States may be efficiently governed by those who are not too scrupulous in their dealings with men or too idealistic in their policy for States.

Asoka, 274 B.C.-237 B.C.—Chandragupta's grandson, Asoka, ascended the throne in 274 B.C. He is known as the Constantine of the East, and in his early life achieved a reputation as a great soldier. He conquered Kalinga, the modern Orissa, in 262 B.C., but the spectacle of the misery and bloodshed caused by war filled him with remorse and he presently became an enthusiastic disciple of Buddha, abjuring violence and preferring peace to military glory.

Asoka carved a number of edicts upon rocks, in which he embodied precepts for the right conduct of human life. These rock-edicts of Asoka, of which thirty-five have been established as definitely authentic, have had an enormous influence upon the moral and religious outlook of subsequent generations of Indians. Asoka was anxious to convert other nations to the Buddhist faith, and sent missionaries to many Eastern and Far Eastern countries. Among these were his son and daughter, Mahendra and Sanghamitra, who converted the king and people of Ceylon to Buddhism. Asoka himself made continuous journeys throughout the length and breadth of India teaching the religion of Buddha and inscribing the doctrines of Ahimsa, a word which may best be translated by the phrase " non-violence and toleration ", upon various pillars and rocks. He died in 237 B.C. and has become a legendary figure in Indian history.

Age of Confusion.—For over five hundred years after Asoka's death (until A.D. 320) India was subjected to constant invasion by the Scythians and Indo-Tartars, who established their dominion over North-western India as far as Rajputana. The dynasty of the Scythian kings, known as the Kusana dynasty, was finally overthrown by the Hindu king, Samudragupta.

King Samudragupta reigned for nearly half a century and brought the whole of Northern India under his rule. His successor, Chandragupta II, was also known as *Vikramaditya*, which means the " Sun of Prowess ". He was an exceedingly civilised king and according to tradition it was at his Court that the Navaratnas, a word which means the " Nine Gems ", that is to say, the nine famous poets and dramatists, flourished. Of these the most famous was Kalidasa.[1] Chandragupta II's capital, Ujjaini, remained for many centuries the centre of Hindu culture. Chandragupta II was succeeded by other famous Gupta emperors, notably Kumaragupta and Skandagupta.

The Gupta Empire. The Golden Age (A.D. 320-470). —It was during the rule of the Gupta emperors that Indian achievement in the realms of art and literature reached its highest level. Apart from the great poet and dramatist, Kalidasa, author of *The Sakuntala* (Princess) and *The Meghaduta* (Cloud Messenger) many other famous literary men flourished during this period. Notable works of the period are the famous frescoes in the Ajanta caves. But many temples, palaces and statues of the most exquisite workmanship have survived.

[1] See Chapter IV, pp. 96, 97.

Toleration and Peace.—The Gupta period was one of prolonged and bitter strife between the Brahminical religion, which was the religion of the original Aryan tribes, and the religion of Buddha. In the end Brahminism triumphed. It succeeded in incorporating most of the essential doctrines of Buddhism and becoming the official faith of India. There seems, however, to have been little persecution as the result of victory. At no time, indeed, in Indian history does the struggle between the Brahminical and Buddhist religions seem to have been characterised by violence or persecution.

Thus Fa-Hien, a Chinese pilgrim who records a visit to Buddhist shrines in India early in the fifth century A.D., testifies to the complete freedom accorded to the Buddhists for the performance of their religious rites. One of the most outstanding characteristics of the period is the scrupulous abstention on the part of both the official religion and the secular Government from interference with the social life of the people. For the greater part of the centuries of Gupta rule there were, if we may trust the literature of the time, neither war nor the fear of war. Peace, which gave security, induced prosperity, and for most of the period during which the Gupta Empire lasted there were established in India the material conditions of a high state of civilisation, the period being often known as "The Golden Age of the Guptas". The Golden Age was brought to an end in the sixth century A.D. by the invasion of the Huns.

A New Age of Confusion.—This inaugurated a

period of political confusion, which lasted for well over a hundred years, and it is not until A.D. 606 that, under King Harsha, ordered government again appears to have been established. According to another Chinese traveller, Hiuen Tsang, Harsha's Empire covered the whole of Northern India, including Rajputana and extending as far as Assam. King Harsha was reported to possess sixty thousand elephants and a hundred thousand cavalry. Harsha was a very pious and devout man, one who, according to Hiuen Tsang "practised to the utmost the rules of temperance, and sought to plant the tree of religious merit to such an extent that he forgot to sleep or eat". Under his rule the two religious sects, Brahmins and Buddhists, professed and practised their religions side by side in what was apparently an amicable tolerance. Harsha himself appears to have enjoyed organising debates between Brahmin and Buddhist priests, and, though his own sympathies were Buddhist, patronised both. Harsha died in A.D. 648. His half century of peace was succeeded by a period of strife. Northern India split up into a number of independent states, among which the Rajput kingdoms, which extended over the greater part of the North of India, attained a predominant position, while in the South various dynasties—the Chalukyas, the Cholas, the Pallavas, the Rashtrakutas—fought for supremacy, which finally went to the Cholas. By A.D. 1000 the Cholas had overrun most of Southern India, and their Empire extended to what are now known as the Kalinga countries on the borders of Northern India.

The Mohammedan Invasion, A.D. 711.—We now come to the period of the Mohammedan invasions. The first of these took place in A.D. 711 and culminated in A.D. 1001, when the celebrated Sultan Mohammed of Ghazni in Afghanistan invaded India. The raids were repeated, and from A.D. 1009 onwards Mohammed is reputed to have raided India on seventeen different occasions. In the end he succeeded in annexing the Punjab. In the twelfth century another invader, Mohammed Ghori, after seventeen years of incessant warfare, succeeded in defeating the Hindu king of Delhi, Prithwiraj, at the battle of Tirouri (1192), Prithwiraj's brother, Joysingh, treacherously going over to the side of the invader.

This final victory by Mohammed Ghori ushered in a period of chaos which lasted for some three hundred years. Massacre, rapine and plunder were almost universal, the invading Moslems considering it to be a duty particularly enjoined upon them by their religion to torture infidels and to destroy their temples. It is for this reason that there are very few temples dating from this period in Northern India.

The Slave Dynasty.—After Ghori's death, his general, Kutb-ud-din, became Emperor of Delhi in 1206. Kutb-ud-din, who was a member of an Afghan tribe on the borders of North-west India, had begun life as a slave, and the dynasty which he founded is consequently known as the Slave, or sometimes as the Pathan,[1] dynasty. The Slave

[1] The word "Pathan" is broadly synonymous with Afghan.

dynasty ruled for eighty-four years, and calls for comment only in respect of the fact that one of its members, Queen Rizia, was a woman. An early feminist, she dressed like a man, rode a horse, led her armies, and was eventually assassinated. After the fall of the Slave dynasty, Ala-ud-din Khilji became Emperor of Northern India about A.D. 1296. He is celebrated in history for the destruction of Chitor, the fortress capital of Mewar which was at that time the leading Rajput kingdom. Of the immediately succeeding emperors the ablest was Mohammed-bin-Tughlak, who extended the frontiers of his Empire as far as Southern India.

The Mogul Empire.—The period which we have so briefly outlined was a veritable period of terror and confusion, and it extended for over five hundred years. Continuously during this period there were insurrections; and continuously the central power became weaker. At last, in the first battle of Panipat in A.D. 1526 the invaders from Central Asia succeeded in completely destroying what remained of the old Empire. Babur, the victor of the battle, became the first of the Mogul emperors, and for a hundred and eighty-one years the Moguls reigned in India. The Mogul period is of the greatest importance in Indian history. During it the continent of India achieved a degree of uniformity such as had not been known for centuries. The Moguls, although invaders and Mohammedans, very rapidly became Indianised. Babur, the first emperor, is, indeed, said to have pined for his homeland in

Central Asia, but his sons and grandsons regarded India as their home and identified themselves with the Indian people.

The Mogul Empire was not without its early vicissitudes; Babur's son Humayun, for example, was defeated by Sher Shah, an Afghan adventurer, and was for sixteen years a fugitive from his kingdom. It was not until 1555, a year before his death, that he regained his throne.

Akbar.—It was only under his son, Akbar (1556-1605) that the Mogul Empire became securely established. Akbar was first and foremost a great conqueror. At the second battle of Panipat in 1556 he defeated the Afghan forces under Himu, and restored the Empire of his father. In 1568 he defeated the Rajput kings, who had allied themselves against him at Chitor, thus making Central India his own, and in 1576 his Hindu general, Man Singh, finally routed the Rajput alliance at the battle of Haldighat, a battle which even to-day occupies a special place in Indian legend because of the reported valour and chivalry of the combatants. Akbar conquered Gujerat in 1573, Bengal in 1576, and Orissa in 1592, and so gradually established his dominion over the whole Indian continent. His position secure, he embarked upon a series of reforms, social, political and religious, for which his reign is chiefly remembered. At Fatepur Sikri he built his capital, a task which occupied him for fifteen years. Although he could not read or write, Akbar had keen intellectual interests, and is said to have taken a particular delight in listening to the competing religious discourses of Hindus, Moslems and Christians. His turn of mind was predominantly speculative, and it was the philosophical implications of Hinduism and Christianity rather than their creeds or ceremonies and rituals which chiefly interested him. Tolerant and broad-minded, he abolished the special taxes imposed by his Mogul predecessors upon the Hindus, threw open all state offices to Hindus and Mohammedans alike, placed Hindus in charge of his armies, and, by a policy of moderation and alliance, secured the friendship of the surviving Hindu states. Akbar was neither a saint nor a philanthropist, but a practical man of strong common sense, whose main concern was to give India just administration and material prosperity. Ruthless when he thought ruthlessness necessary, he was in general mild and moderate. Now mildness and moderation are rare qualities in all men; in those who possess great power they are doubly rare. They are the greatest adornments of a ruler, in proportion as they are the most difficult of attainment.

After Akbar's death, his son, Jehangir, ruled India from 1605 to 1627. Under Jehangir, the Mogul Empire began to decline. It was during his reign that the first English Ambassador, Sir Thomas Roe, was received at the Mogul Court.

Jehangir's elder son, Shah Jehan, ascended the throne in 1627, and ruled until 1658 when he was made a prisoner by his son Aurangzeb. Shah Jehan caused many beautiful buildings to be constructed of which the Taj Mahal is the most famous.

Aurangzeb, the last of the great Moguls, ruled from 1659 to 1707. Like all the Moguls, he was a Mohammedan, but unlike some of his predecessors he was a bigoted Mohammedan. He persecuted the Hindus, aroused violent opposition, carried out wars of conquest in different parts of India which were not always successful, and exhausted the resources of the Empire. During his reign there appeared in Western India a new power under the leadership of Sivaji, the king of the Mahrattas.

The Coming of the English.—In 1639 the East India Company, founded in 1600 with a charter from Queen Elizabeth, had established itself in Madras and had purchased from Charles II the town of Bombay, which Charles had acquired as part of the dowry of his Portuguese wife, Catherine of Braganza. Calcutta was founded by Job Charnock in North-eastern India in 1690.

After the death of Aurangzeb the political predominance of the Moguls still further declined, and during the eighteenth century India was continually devastated by wars in which the Mahrattas, a warlike people from Western India who had been organised into a military power by Sivaji in the sixteenth century, the Sikhs from the North-west under the leadership of Guru Govind Singh, the French and the English, struggled for supremacy.

In 1739, Nadir Shah of Persia raided Delhi, and in 1761 Ahmad Shah Durani defeated the Mahrattas at the third battle of Panipat. During the next thirty years Sikhs and Mohammedans were busy fighting each other and by the end of the century the Mahrattas had become the most important non-European power in India.

Growth of British Power.—Meanwhile in Bengal the tyrannical rule of the independent Prince Siraju-d-dowlah had aroused discontent. The army, the feudal landlords and the bankers, conspired to overthrow him, and brought Robert Clive, an officer of the East India Company, into their conspiracy. With the help of the discontented army, Clive succeeded in driving out the Nawab, and installed Mir Jafar in his place. From Mir Jafar Clive obtained valuable concessions for himself and for the East India Company. Thus established in India, the British for a hundred years pursued a policy in which war, alliance and annexation were astutely blended. By 1858 practically the whole of India had been brought within the British sphere of influence.

The Indian Mutiny.—In 1858 the Indian Army rebelled against the British. Their cause was supported by the discontented and disinherited nobility, but the Indian Mutiny, as it was called, failed to assume a complete national character. During the last hundred years of British dominance a powerful middle class had grown up in India. The members of this class valued security and prosperity above all other goods, and threw their weight into the scale on the side of the existing order—that is to say, the order which was maintained by the British. British policy exploited to its own advantage the traditional animosity of Hindus against Moslems, and within a few months the English succeeded in entirely suppressing the rebellion. In 1858 the government of India was transferred from the East India Company to the British Crown.

Indian Nationalism.—During the last seventy years there has grown up in India a powerful nationalist movement. The more extreme sections of this movement demand complete independence for India. The more moderate would be content with Home Rule within the British Empire such as is accorded, for example, to South Africa or to Australia. It seems unlikely that even this degree of independence will be achieved in the near future. The British Government, it is true, have recently drawn up a new constitution for India, but the measure of independence which it accords falls so far short of Home Rule and leaves so much power in British hands, that many Indians are in doubt as to whether they should do their best to "work" the constitution on the principle that any concession should be eagerly seized, or whether they should refuse to co-operate with the British in the government of India. The future of India at the moment of writing is thus very uncertain.[1]

§ 2. The Mingling of Races

The Multitude of Races.—The foregoing brief sketch of Indian history will have served its purpose, if it brings home to the reader a realisation of the frequency with which India has been invaded, and of

[1] Some of the questions involved are briefly discussed at the end of Chapter V. See pp. 124-126.

the number and variety of the strains that are in consequence blended in the present population of the country. From the earliest beginnings of recorded history, millions of people, for the most part fair-skinned people, have been pouring into India through the North-western passes and mingling their blood with that of the original inhabitants, who were usually darker in complexion. Of these peoples the most important were the Vedic Aryans. Since the time when they first invaded India, over three thousand years ago, it is they, more than any other race who have dominated Indian history, and, it is their ideas which chiefly determine the character of Indian social, religious and political institutions to-day. Nevertheless, the Aryan is far from being the sole strand in the complex fabric of modern India. From the very first, the Aryan strain mingled with others. Later it incorporated yet others, and to-day whatever is Indian, whether it be an idea, a creed, a form of art, a political institution, or a social custom, is a blend of many different elements.

The Tolerance of the Aryans.—It is not immediately obvious why those who worship a particular kind of God in a particular kind of way, hold particular beliefs about the nature of this universe in which we find ourselves, or wish to live a particular kind of life, and to regulate the affairs of their community by a particular code of law—it is not immediately obvious, I say, why they should wish everybody else to worship the same God in the same way, to hold the same sort of beliefs, to live the same kind of life, to be regulated by the same code of law. Nevertheless, it is by precisely this wish that almost all the human beings who have ever lived have been animated. As a result, an acquiescence in the continuance of the laws, beliefs and customs of defeated peoples by their victors is a comparatively rare event in history, the victors having usually insisted upon those whom they have defeated behaving and believing as they do themselves. It may be taken, then, more or less for granted in the history of mankind that the manners, customs, thoughts, values, tastes and beliefs of conquered or incorporated peoples should be persecuted and suppressed.

Now, in India they have on the whole not been persecuted and suppressed. Why is this? Why, for example, were the indigenous inhabitants of India tolerated by the early Aryans? For the early Aryans, we must suppose, after they had conquered, settled down in India and taken stock of their surroundings, decided that certain features in the life and thought of the existing inhabitants were such as they could accept or at any rate adapt, and, surprisingly, accepted and adapted them. Why, almost alone among early peoples, they should have been willing to perform this, surely not very difficult feat, we cannot tell. It may have been simply that they possessed that extremely rare quality, a tolerance for what was other than their own. It may have been that they were distinguished by something still rarer, so rare among men as to be almost unique—an ability to recognise and a willingness to follow what was good, simply because it was good.

Whatever the reason, it is a fact that India's special gift to mankind has been the ability and willingness of Indians to effect a synthesis of many different elements both of thoughts and of peoples, to create, in fact, unity out of diversity.[1]

This unifying tendency is already noticeable in the earliest hymns of the *Rig Veda*; it animates the religious teachings of Indian teachers and thinkers of all ages; it is apparent in the acts and edicts of many of India's rulers and their advisers. The number of wars by which India has been devastated is not much less than those which ravaged the continent of Europe. Nevertheless, there has rarely been a period in India's history when there have not been multitudes of Indians advocating the practice of non-violence and putting in the forefront of their lives the ideals of toleration and unity. The practice of non-violence is still, to-day, a distinguishing feature of India's political methods.

The Races of India.—The following is a brief summary of the races and of the main characteristics of the races which have gone to the making of India.

1. *The Indo-Aryan.* The Indo-Aryan stock is met with chiefly in the Punjab, in Kashmir and in Rajputana. It is particularly prevalent among the higher castes in Northern India. The Indo-Aryans are a tall, slight, and loose-limbed people with long prominent noses and light brown complexions.

2. *The Dravidian.* The Dravidian stock is chiefly met with in Southern India. The typical

[1] See Chapter II, pp. 27, 28 and 45-49, for a general account of the philosophical doctrine of unity in diversity.

Dravidian is a short, dark man with long black hair, a broad nose and wide, rather flattish, nostrils.

3. *Mongolian.* The Mongolians are chiefly found among the races inhabiting the borderland between India and Thibet, Assam and Burma. They are small men with broad heads, narrow slanting eyes, dark or yellow complexions and flat faces.

These are the main stocks from which the diverse peoples of India are chiefly sprung. Four subsidiary types which have also been distinguished are formed from an admixture of these stocks, together with elements drawn in some cases from other peoples. These four mixed races are:

1. *Aryo-Dravidian, or Hindustani.* These are found in the United Provinces, in parts of Rajputana and in Bihar. They appear to be the result of the intermixture in varying proportions of the Indo-Aryan and Dravidian stocks. Their heads are long, their complexions vary from lightish-brown to black, their noses from medium to broad. They are, however, always broader than the noses of the pure Indo-Aryans.

2. *Mongolo-Dravidian.* These mainly inhabit lower Bengal, Orissa and Assam. They are, as their name suggests, a blend of Dravidian and Mongoloid elements, enriched in the higher classes by Indo-Aryan blood. Their outstanding characteristics are broad heads, dark complexions and plentiful hair. Their stature is medium.

3. *The Scytho-Dravidian.* This mixed race is found in the Mahratta countries, in North-west India, and in Rajputana. It is probably the result

of the mixture of Scythian and Dravidian elements. Low stature, long heads, and short noses are the outstanding characteristics of this race.

4. *Turco-Iranian.* The Turco-Iranian race is found in Beluchistan and in the North-west Frontier Provinces. Its members seem to be the result of a fusion of Turkish and Persian elements. They are fair-complexioned and tall, with long noses and broad heads.

The above classification is a rough one, and affords only a very general guide to the distribution of the Indian races. For centuries there have been continuous migrations from one part of the country to the other, with the result that all kinds of odd types appear in the most unexpected regions. There is a general tendency for Indians of the higher castes, and in particular those of the Brahmin caste, to have fairer skins and lighter hair than the average. They claim that these characteristics are due to the fact that they have a larger share of Aryan blood. Indians, however, who are no less fair and light than the Brahmins, are found in lower castes and frequently appear amongst the generally dark-skinned Tamils of the south. At any moment, in fact, one may meet people of an obviously Indo-Aryan or an obviously Dravidian type in any part of India and in any caste.

Results of the Mingling of Races.—This admixture of races has had important effects on India's past history and present outlook. The first of these is a sense of fundamental unity far more vivid and persistent than can be accounted for by the circumstance of propinquity in the same geographical area. Europeans live together in a geographical area whose size is not very different from that of India. But as the wars which have disgraced European history in the past and the quarrels and rivalries that enfeeble the League of Nations in the present only too clearly show, the inhabitants of Europe are very far from being imbued with the sense of unity which distinguishes the inhabitants of India. We cannot, in short, speak of "a European" with the same appropriateness as we can speak of "an Indian", who, in spite of differences of colour, caste and creed, looks upon all other Indians as his fellow-countrymen and upon India as his home.

The case of the Mohammedans affords a particularly good example of the process of Indianisation at work. The Mohammedans came to India as invaders, invaders who established an empire. In a very short space of time, however, they became absorbed in the country they had conquered, and in spite of a deliberate attempt to foster an extra-territorial patriotism amongst Moslems as a whole, the large majority of Indian Moslems identify themselves as completely with other Indians as an Englishman does with other Englishmen.

Toleration.—To a second outstanding effect of the mingling of races I have already referred. This is the toleration of other people's habits, customs and faiths which, I have insisted, is so unusual a feature in the history of mankind. An average Indian takes it instinctively for granted that everybody is entitled to his own point of view, that between different men and different races of men differences of taste, habit, thought and religion are inevitable, and that these should neither be resented nor obliterated. There are, of course, in India rigid barriers of caste, but there is not, as a general rule, dislike of or disdain for men of a different religion, culture or habit from one's own. Tolerance for the cultivated Indian is, indeed, no less enjoined by good manners than dictated by good sense.

Acceptance of Foreigners.—In the third place, it may be conjectured that it is largely because of the many strains in their own blood that Indians, unlike many other peoples, feel entirely at their ease with foreigners, and do not, as a general rule, cherish any prejudice against them. Successive invasions have made the Indians aware of foreigners. Foreigners exist; they are a fact, and inevitably their faces, their language, their religion and their habits are odd. The Indian accepts the fact, and does not resent it. He bears no animosity against a man because he looks and thinks differently from himself. This, no doubt, seems a reasonable attitude enough—one expects a foreigner to be different and recognises that he cannot help his difference. Few human beings have, however, been able to adopt it.

To sum up, the mixture of races has widened the outlook of Indians, made them receptive of new impressions and accustomed them to the impact of new ideas. As a result, they are cosmopolitan in outlook, tolerant in behaviour and open-minded in thought. In the succeeding pages we shall find that events in India afford much reason for criticism and some occasion for regret. Let us, then, at the beginning of this book, pay tribute to these great virtues which have distinguished Indians from the outset of their history—the virtues of unity, of tolerance and of open-mindedness.

CHAPTER II

THE SEARCH FOR TRUTH AND PERFECTION. PHILOSOPHY AND RELIGION

Characteristics of Indian Philosophy.—Perhaps the most outstanding achievement of Indian civilisation is Indian philosophy, or rather Indian philosophy and Indian religion, for, as we shall shortly see, these two phases of the activity of the human spirit, the speculative and the receptive, the one which explores the universe and the other which responds to it, in Europe distinct and at times even opposed, are in India frequently indistinguishable. I propose, therefore, to include both philosophy and religion under the title of this chapter.

Indian philosophy is quite unlike that of any other people; it is distinguished by three characteristics. The first is continuity. Indian thinkers have been enquiring into the nature and meaning of the universe more or less continuously for a period of some three thousand years. Only the Chinese can show a similar record. The second is unanimity. Broadly speaking, all Indian thinkers have concurred in holding that the universe in its real nature is in an important sense a unity, and that this unity is spiritual. Now the universe, as it appears, is certainly not a unity but a heterogeneous diversity. It contains, that is to say—

it apparently *is*—a collection of an enormous number of people and things. Hence, there must be a distinction between the universe as it really is and the universe as it appears, a distinction which may be expressed by saying that the universe is a reality which manifests itself in diversity, just as the *leit motif* or underlying theme of a piece of music manifests itself in the diversity of individual notes which all express the same musical idea. Now, it is broadly true that all Indian thinkers have concurred in making this distinction. Thirdly—and here we come to the link between philosophy and religion—Indian philosophy has never been confined to the activity of the intellect. Formally, no doubt, it is a search for truth; but philosophy in India does more than search for truth; it also seeks and prescribes a way of life. In fact, in the last resort it *is* a way of life, a way of life as well as a way of believing. This practical effect of Indian philosophy follows inevitably from the doctrines of Indian philosophers.

Philosophy and Life.—Indian philosophy teaches that life has a meaning and a goal; it is our duty to discover the meaning and our privilege ultimately to attain the goal. Philosophy, therefore, which seeks to reveal the meaning, constitutes, in so far as it succeeds, an advance towards the goal. For what, after all, is the goal? The attainment of reality in the sense in which to attain is not only to know, but to become one with. What impedes this attainment? There are many impediments, but among the chief is ignorance. The uninstructed soul does not know that the world of apparent "many" is not the only, is not even the real, world. It is philosophy which instructs him and by its instruction confers emancipation (Moksha) from the ignorance (Avidya) which conceals the vision of reality. Thus philosophy is not only a key to knowledge but a pathway to reality. To follow this pathway is not only to know, but to strive, and, if the striving is successful, ultimately to *be*. Thus to be a philosopher is to follow not only an intellectual but a vital discipline. For the good philosopher, engaged on the quest for reality, is required so to conduct his life, that he may be led to become one with the reality he seeks. There is, in fact, one way of life which is a right way, and this all philosophers are required to follow: and not only all philosophers, but all men, for the duty and the destiny of all men are the same.

The Four Stages.—This way of life consists of four stages, namely: (1) Brahmacharya, or the period of training, (2) Garhastya, or the period of work as a householder, (3) Vanaprasthya, or the period of gradual retirement, and (4) Sanyasa, or the period of preparation when what is misleadingly called death, which is the emancipation of the soul from ignorance and desire, is tranquilly awaited. Life, in fact, is a pilgrimage; there are four stages on the road, and the end which is called death is but a gateway to an eternal life. Just as there are four stages in life, so are there four goods or values which a life rightly lived will embody. To have achieved each of these goods in its appropriate degree is the object of a life well-lived. The goods in question are (1) Dharma, (2) Artha, (3) Kama, and (4) Moksha.

Dharma is right action—that is to say, action which is in conformity with the nature of things. This distinctively Hindu conception does not admit of summary description. Broadly, however, the intention of Dharma is to insist upon the desirability of a life in which all the sides or aspects of the soul of man are properly integrated. I have spoken hitherto, as if the worlds of appearance and reality were two worlds, even as if they were in some sense opposed worlds. This is not, however, the case.

The world of reality is *expressed* in the world of appearance, and the real or spiritual nature of man is similarly *expressed* in his apparent or human nature. In a life badly lived these two natures, the real and the apparent, may turn against each other, and, though we cannot altogether extinguish our spiritual natures, yet by developing and concentrating upon our purely earthly desires, we may overlay them and drive them, as it were, into the background of our conscious being. This is to subordinate the higher nature to the lower, the greater value to the less, the real to the apparent; in a word, it is the wrong way of life. The prescribed method of avoiding this error is continuously to relate our lives to the background of the underlying reality in which they are cast; to live our lives, as we should say in the West, under the shadow of eternity. Dharma is the way of life which observes this relation and keeps it constantly in mind; it prescribes, that is to say, a right relation between the temporal and the earthly on the one hand and the eternal and the spiritual on the other.

Artha is the discipline which acknowledges the needs of the economic and the political life of man. Prescribing the pursuit of wealth as legitimate, it insists that the law of righteousness (Dharma) must be observed, if we are to achieve the final end of life, which is Moksha, or salvation. A similar caveat attaches to the Hindu teaching in regard to Kama (pleasure). That pleasure is a good is recognised, and its pursuit is encouraged. But its enjoyment must be always such as is compatible with the ultimate spiritual nature of man; pleasure must, that is to say, be subordinated to the achievement of man's ultimate good, which is spiritual freedom. In point of fact, most Indian religion is markedly ascetic in character. Pleasures in general and bodily pleasures in particular are regarded as belonging in a quite peculiar degree to the world of appearance, and indulgence in pleasure is censured on the ground that it roots the soul more firmly in the world, subjects it to the craving of desire, and perpetuates the train of causes and effects which rivet more firmly upon the individual the chains of his bondage to the law of Karma.[1]

As Indian philosophy develops, writer after writer insists that emancipation from ignorance, and the world of appearance, which is the correlative of ignorance, is the end of life. To achieve this end the soul must submit itself to ethical discipline. If man's real life is the life of the spirit, the most that can be expected of his everyday activity is that it should impede as little as possible the development of the

[1] See pp. 53-55 below.

spirit and conduce to its ultimate emancipation (Moksha), that is to say, to the departure of the self from the world of appearance, its freeing from the craving of desire, and the fulfilment of its true spiritual nature in unity with the reality of which it is an aspect.

Philosophy and Religion.—But philosophy was for the Hindu sage no less a mode of belief, than a way of life. Bound up with morals, it forms no less an integral part of religion. The Hindu attitude to religion has been dominated throughout by the doctrines contained in the Vedas and the Upanishads, more especially in the form in which they were subsequently developed by the philosopher Sankara.[1] Hindu philosophers, in fact, were often called seers, the Sanskrit word for philosophy being Darsana, which may be translated "seeing". Granted that reality is such as Hindu thought conceived it to be, it is not difficult to see why the quest for it should be regarded as a religious duty, why, in fact, the pursuit of philosophy should become one with the observance of religion. Yet this ultimate identity of the two activities is a conception alien to the Westerner, alien because religion itself is by him differently conceived. For the Westerner, a religion is a body of doctrine consisting of certain affirmations about the nature of the universe and about God, the creator of the universe, divinely revealed to the mind of the believer and, therefore, absolutely and eternally true. From the assurance that the doctrines of any particular religion are absolutely and

[1] See pp. 50-53 below.

eternally true, it follows that the doctrines of any other religion, in so far as they differ from them, cannot be true. Hence the persecution and intolerance which have so continuously accompanied the practice of religion in the West are in a large part the offspring of the persecutors' conviction of the absolute truth of the beliefs in the interests of which he has persecuted, and of the wickedness of the contrary beliefs which he has sought to stamp out.

Now Indian philosophy, while teaching that reality is spiritual and is one, was not prepared to make a detailed and dogmatic specification of the nature of "the One". In the absence of detailed and dogmatic specification, men were at liberty to conceive it very much as they pleased. Thus while the priests and philosophers conceived austerely of Brahman as a single unity or absolute, which only by a gross anthropomorphism could be personified as God, popular Hindu religion made no difficulty about representing the Brahman, not as a single God but as three. The celebrated Hindu Trinity—Brahma, the God of Creation, Vishnu, the God of Preservation, and Siva, the God of Destruction—are at one and the same time independent deities, living emanations from the Brahman, and phases or aspects under which the Brahman may be conceived—a very illuminating example of unity in difference!

The diversity of these conceptions of the infinite and ultimate One is, however, given the fundamental pre-suppositions of Indian philosophy, readily intelligible. Since no definite affirmation stood much chance of being absolutely true, a number might well be regarded as all embodying some degree of truth. Just as the world was a unity of reality manifesting itself in many different appearances, so religion was a unity of truth expressing itself in many different creeds. Truth, in fact, no less than reality, illustrated the all-pervasive principle of Hindu philosophy, the principle of unity in difference. Thus the doctrines of Hinduism were never reduced to a set of formal creeds and Hindu religion has always been willing to receive new experiences and to incorporate new knowledge. Believing that man's knowledge and understanding of reality evolves, the Hindu sage has been in a position to accept, even to welcome, new religious conceptions. Thus a multitude of different tribal creeds have at different times been incorporated into the body of Hindu religious thought. To this fact is due the bewildering variety of Indian religions, a variety which ranges from the open polytheism of the masses to the rigid and uncompromising monotheism of the elect. And the justification for this complexity of heterogeneous, of even contradictory doctrines, is precisely the foundation theme of all Indian philosophy, namely, that since truth and reality are one, every creed is a product of man's insight at different levels into the same truth about the same reality.

Philosophy and Ethics.—But at this point the single-piece garment of Indian thought, which already covers philosophy and religion, is extended to embrace ethics; for just because belief is comparatively unimportant, conduct is all-important. Reality, as we have seen, is one, and reality is spirit. The world of things extended in space is, therefore, an appearance only. To which world does man belong, to reality or appearance? The answer is to both. There is in man a spiritual principle, the principle of reality, which, imprisoned in the flesh, is confused by desire and darkened by ignorance. By following the right way of life man can, as we have seen, overcome the barriers that obscure and impede the workings of the spirit, and realise his true nature, which is also his spiritual nature. Religion, which lays down this realisation of his true nature as man's end, enjoins also the conduct which is necessary to achieve this end. While insisting, that is to say, that the end of life is spiritual fulfilment, it indicates the road which must be followed, if the end is to be achieved; and, since it is only to the man who lives rightly that truth is revealed, the apprehension of the truth which is sought by philosophy no less than the realisation of the end which is enjoined by religion depends primarily upon conduct. In other words, it is by living rightly that we come to have right views and practice necessarily precedes and determines theory. Hinduism is thus less a religion in the Western sense of the word than a fellowship of all of those who accept the immutable laws of right conduct and fashion their lives after the pattern whose lines philosophy, religion and ethics have combined to trace. To sum up this doctrine in a famous Western phrase, it is not by faith but by works that man is saved.

What is meant by "works" and what by "saved"? The answer to this question leads us to a more detailed consideration of some of the basic ideas of Indian philosophy.

Before, however, we are in a position to undertake it, there is one further application of the all-pervasive doctrine of reality as a unity in diversity which remains to be described, namely, its application in the social and political spheres. The following out of this application entails a brief treatment of the vexed question of castes.

Digression on the Caste System.—The inclusion of an account of the caste system and of the purposes which it was intended to serve in a Chapter on Indian philosophy seems at first sight to call for some explanation. The subject is, however, introduced deliberately at this stage, because it serves to throw into relief that continuity between Indian thought and practice upon which I have already sought to lay emphasis, and is, in fact, the concrete embodiment in the structure of Indian society of that unity in diversity which I have exhibited as the basic principle of Indian thought. From the time when the first Aryan settlers founded a colony on the banks of the Indus in the dawn of history, India has been faced with the problem of creating a system which would include in a single social unity the diverse races and peoples in various stages of growth and at different levels of civilisation who from time to time came to make their home in the continent of India.

The caste system was a creation of the Aryans. In their onward march through the length and breadth of India the Aryans came into contact with the Dravidians and other half-civilised peoples living in hills and forests of the southern part of the continent. These in due course they subdued; but subjugation was not enough. How, they asked themselves, were they to harmonise in a single social whole so many diverse racial elements, how blend so many different traditions, rituals and customs into a single culture and a single religion ? The answer to that question is, broadly speaking, by the caste system, the most striking of all the syntheses of Hindu thought and practice.

Contemporary Criticism of the Caste System.—The caste system is to-day a by-word for snobbery and injustice. It is, Europeans affirm, the caste system that makes one Indian despise another, not for any fault in the man despised, but for the misfortune of his birth. It is the caste system which determines a man's lot in life by an accident over which he has no control, the accident of the bedroom in which he happens to have been born. It is the caste system which permits men to develop a complacent superiority whose arrogance cannot be matched anywhere in the world, and which is responsible for that supreme outrage upon humanity, the segregation of fifty-four million people as humanly untouchable. That there is substance in these common charges of the West few educated Indians would, I think, wish to deny. Such, at any rate, as I have met—and I have no reason to suppose them to be unrepresentative—

regard the thing which the caste system has become with feelings of unmixed repulsion. But what it has become is something very different from what in intention it was; nor should we allow dislike of its contemporary vices to blind us to the difficulties which it was designed to meet, and to its considerable early success in meeting them.

Origin and Justification of the Caste System.—From the very beginning of its history, India, as we have seen, has been a dumping ground upon which uncountable multitudes of different peoples have been deposited by the action of those far-flung forces which determined the migrations of early man. At widely different levels of culture and civilisation these peoples brought with them into India different religions, different customs and different laws. How were they to be assimilated? How, out of such a diverse heterogeneity of blood and colour and language and custom and belief was a single social and political entity to be formed? Broadly speaking, three courses were open. The first was the abandonment of any attempt to achieve unity. Had this course been followed, India would have remained a chaos of warring peoples. The second was to impose uniformity by oppression and, if necessary, by extermination. Besides being repugnant to morals, this would have weakened the whole by eliminating or impoverishing its integral parts. The third course was that of harmonisation. It seemed possible, that is to say, to attempt to integrate these many different races, to co-ordinate these many different civilisations into a single whole, a whole which, nevertheless, allowed full scope for the development of the characteristics of its component individual parts. In other words—and here we may pause to note the illustration of our main theme—there was the policy of applying to the workings of human society the philosophical principle of unity in difference. This was the policy adopted and the caste system was its result. Before, then, we subscribe, as we must do, to its condemnation by the contemporary world, let us remember that in origin and intention, at least, this justly denounced system was nothing more nor less than a device for enabling different races to live together in harmony, so that the unity which was constituted by what all had in common should be continuously developed by what each contributed from the background of its individual differences. Inevitably, the highest common factor of all must form the unity; but the human spirit blossoms in many diverse ways, and this highest common factor was enriched by incorporating the fruits of diversity. It is well to remember, secondly, that it is partly because of the caste system that India has in some measure escaped the series of internecine wars which have disgraced the continent of Europe. In Europe, too, there is a multitude of different races; in Europe, too, there exists a basis for a unity of religion and culture. No such unity has been achieved. Europe is not a single society which exhibits a unity in diversity. It is a congeries of different Nation-States, whose jealousies and pride, whose fears and suspicions, have effectively militated against any common action for the common good, and are at the moment endangering the very existence of such civilisation as Europe has been able to achieve.

The Workings of the System.—Originally the caste system appears to have been based upon differences of colour. Later, differences of function became the basis of division. The resultant grading of classes by occupation produced a society similar to that commended by Plato in his *Republic* and embodying the essence of Plato's definition of Justice, in that the members of each caste, the followers of each occupation, knew and attended to their own business and did not aspire to perform the functions of members of different castes.

The Brahmins, the highest caste, consisted of a hierarchy of priests. Like the Guardians in Plato's State, they were the preservers of communal tradition. Unaffected by family ties, uninfluenced by the thought of personal gain, they were expected to direct the affairs of the community without seeking to promote their private interests.

The Kshatriyas, the counterpart of Plato's warrior class, dedicated themselves to the cultivation of physical fitness and military prowess. They were the guardians of the peace of society, and were entrusted with the task of checking the lawlessness of its anti-social elements. Many important State offices were reserved for the Kshatriyas, who constituted what we should now call the executive class. The so-called economic group consisted of the Vaisyas or traders. These were enjoined by the traditions of the system to suppress private greed, and to consider their wealth as a social trust which would enable them to assume responsibility for the maintenance of the economic life of society. The fourth caste, consisting of the Sudras, or unskilled workers, formed the proletariat of the nation, the responsibility for whose maintenance rested in theory upon the other three groups.

Originally the castes were elastic, and the fact that families could pass from caste to caste increased the willingness of all castes to work together for the preservation of the system and the society it supported. It was their sense of being members of a common whole which for centuries precluded the occurrence among Indians of anything in the nature of what modern Europe knows as class conflict. As well might the members of the whole which is the human body engage in combat against one another, the heart against the lungs or the brain against the feet. At its best the system may be reckoned as one of the most successful attempts to maintain harmony between different races and creeds living together in geographical propinquity that the world has seen.

The System Degenerates.—By the time Buddha was born (*circa* 563 B.C.) the system was already tending to degenerate into a hard and rigid framework which perpetuated inequality and put a premium upon snobbery. Its main interest for us lies in the fact that in its early stages it represents one of the most successful applications of a philosophic principle to the world of concrete fact that mankind has contrived. This principle, the underlying principle of Indian philosophy, was that of unity in diversity which the caste system showed operating in action and operating successfully in action.

Form of Indian Philosophy.—What has hitherto been written constitutes rather an introduction to Indian philosophy than an account of it. I have spoken of its continuity, of its relation to religion and conduct, of its conception of reality as a unity in diversity and of the application of that conception to the structure of society. It remains to give a brief account of its form and content. The form is peculiar. There is, indeed, nothing analogous to it in the thought of any other people. For Indian philosophy is made up, not of the systems of independent and original thinkers, but of certain books of sacred writings of a theological character and of the commentaries which subsequent scholars have made upon them. The form of Indian philosophical systems varies very little. There is a set of poems or prose aphorisms, the Vedas or the Upanishads, from which the system derives and upon which it is based. There are treatises written in short pregnant sentences, the Sutras, usually in commentary upon or exposition of the original poems or of the ideas contained in them. The Sutras, being held in the greatest respect, any new thought or speculation which occurs to subsequent thinkers is announced in the form of a commentary upon or development of the thought of the Sutras. It has, therefore, first to be reconciled with them, in the sense of being shown to be merely a development of ideas already latent in them, and secondly, to defend itself against the criticism of rival systems. In this way, the original poems, the Sutras, and the commentaries upon and developments of the Sutras come to form an elaborate system. As the system grows, it has to meet unexpected criticisms, and to withstand the impact of new ideas for which it is not in the least prepared. Thus, in the words of Professor Dasgupta, each system "grew and developed by the untiring energy of its adherents through all the successive ages of history; and a history of this growth is a history of its conflicts".[1]

The process I have recorded is quite unlike anything in Western thought. The original poems and prose aphorisms consist of philosophical truths intuitively perceived, revelations of reality, which are considered to need neither argument nor defence. The Sutras are more like lecture notes than books; short and pithy, they bristle with technical terms and are full of allusions to the objections brought by rival systems which they are seeking to refute. Not only are the technical terms not explained, but they are used in different senses in different places, while the allusions, intelligible enough to those who, no doubt, had direct oral instruction on the subject, are lost upon modern readers.

Puzzled by the form of Indian philosophy, the Westerner is unable to see why it should have been adopted. Is it not, he cannot help wondering, prejudicial to new thought to compel it to accommodate itself within the bounds of a traditional system?

[1] Quoted from *A History of Indian Philosophy* by Surendranath Dasgupta.

Does not the religious veneration with which the systems are regarded as complete compendia of truth tend to stifle free enquiry, and to substitute scholarship and textual criticism, dialectical skill and the ingenuity which is required of those who must fit new pieces into old frameworks, for the free play of the unfettered mind? The Westerner finds the implied criticism of these reflections confirmed by the following quotation from Professor Dasgupta's *A History of Indian Philosophy*:

> "All the independence of their thinking was limited and enchained by the faith of the school to which they were attached. Instead of producing a succession of free-lance thinkers having their own systems to propound and establish, India had brought forth schools of pupils who carried the traditionary views of particular systems from generation to generation, who explained and expounded them, and defended them against the attacks of other rival schools which they constantly attacked in order to establish the superiority of the system to which they adhered."

The history of the systems extends for about two thousand years. Their development seems to have stopped about the beginning of the seventeenth century, and with the development of the systems Indian philosophy itself seems to have come to a standstill. Within these systems there occurs, embedded in a mass of philosophically irrelevant and often unintelligible matter, practically every philosophical idea which has at various times occurred to the Western mind from the days of Socrates to the twentieth century. The mode of presentation has, however, proved such a stumbling block to Europeans that Indian thought still remains largely unknown, its value still largely unsuspected by Western thinkers.

Chronological Outline of Indian Philosophy.—The following very brief sketch outlines the main course of this remarkable growth. The Vedas, as we have seen in the first chapter, are among the earliest Indian writings. They consist of directions for religious ritual and ceremonial and occasionally of aphorisms relating to conduct. Their philosophical content, though small, includes a number of bold and original speculations with regard to the origin of the world and the nature of God. In some of the hymns of the *Rig-Veda* and the *Atharva-Veda*, there appears for the first time what might be justifiably termed philosophical argument as distinct from apocalyptic assertion.

The Upanishads.—The doctrines of the Vedas are presented in a more developed form in the Upanishads. The thought of the Upanishads is bold and free, and their general conclusion is that mystical experience is the pathway to reality. The Upanishads are, however, by no means exclusively mystical. On the more strictly philosophical side they issue in conclusions which are not very different from those which the West knows as monist or objective idealist.

In the *Kenopanishad*, the Brahman, or the Supreme Being, is described as one who is beyond the reach of words or thought. He is, however, declared to be both the final source of all the powers in the world and the ultimate ground of all the features of the world. It is from Him, for example, that the gods derive their powers, while in Him the difference between the subject and object of knowledge disappears. Inevitably the nature of the Brahman is different from that of anything that is known; it is also different from all that is unknown. But although beyond the reach of sensuous experience and logical thought, the Brahman may, it is hinted, be realised in mystical experience.

The *Kathopanishad* gives a further account of the Brahman. He is all-pervading and invisible and is yet hidden deep within the human heart. He is in fact the inmost essence of man's soul. This inmost essence, this real nature of man, is eternal and imperishable, and cannot, therefore, be affected by any of the changes that occur in the mind or the body. Thus the true self of man is eternal and continuous with the ultimate reality or essence of the unknown reality.

Basic Doctrines of Indian Philosophy.—In these several writings we come for the first time upon a clear statement of the central doctrines of Indian philosophy. For convenience, I summarise them in the form of a series of propositions.

1. The reality of the universe is a spiritual unity.
2. This spiritual unity is expressed or manifested in everything.
3. It is, therefore, expressed or manifested in the true being of man.
4. Man in his true being is, therefore, one not only with other men, but with the ultimate reality of the universe.

5. There is a distinction, then, between the true being of man and what is sometimes spoken of as his apparent nature. This apparent nature, together with everything else that *appears* to be, is also necessarily a manifestation of the Brahman, since the Brahman is everything. But it is a manifestation at a different level. It is in fact to be regarded as *Maya*, a distinctively Indian conception, of which some account is given below.

The basic ideas summarised in these propositions appear in various forms in the other Upanishads, which may be compared to a number of variations on the same musical theme.

The Other Upanishads.—Thus the *Prasna Upanishad*, which devotes its attention primarily to the individual human being, describes him as a bio-psychological entity composed of sixteen parts, all of which derive from a central indestructible self. The sixteen parts of the bio-psychological individual are ultimately merged in the true self, as the waters of a river are merged in the ocean.

The *Mundaka Upanishad* speaks of two sciences and two selves—the lower and the higher. The lower science consists of the study of the Vedas only, whereas the higher science is directed to the study and ultimate realisation of the imperishable reality. The higher self is free and pure, and the lower is in bondage. When the lower self recognises the higher self as its lord, it becomes free. Another feature of the *Mundaka Upanishad* is its account of the creation of the world. The world is nothing more nor less than an emanation from the Brahman. The Brahman is omniscient and omnipotent, yet as we have seen, he resides in the heart of man as his true self. This true self, which is also the Brahman, can be realised only through the dawn of spiritual illumination.

The distinctive feature of the *Taittiriya Upanishad* is the emphasis which it lays upon the nature of the Brahman as pure blissfulness. It is from this blissfulness that the whole world, both of conscious and unconscious being, has sprung. The *Chandogya Upanishad* again represents the Brahman as the ultimate reality from which everything is educed and to which everything ultimately returns. It also endeavours to throw some light upon the peculiarly baffling problem of the relation between the Brahman and His manifestations in the world of appearance. The Brahman is obviously in some sense the cause of the world of appearance in which He is manifested, and the object of the *Chandogya Upanishad* is by means of an analysis of the concepts of cause and effect to emphasise the essential quality of the Brahman, the cause, and the purely formal character of the world, the effect. The effect, the world of appearance, is, it is affirmed, a mere name or form. Thus the view that the Brahman, the ultimate cause, is the only reality is maintained, and its manifestations are stigmatised as being merely appearances. In the *Brhadaranyaka Upanishad*, the continuity of being between the true self of man and reality is again emphasised, and, since the Brahman is bliss, the corollary is drawn that, by the discovery of the true self one attains to true bliss. The *Brhadaranyaka Upanishad* also throws a little more light upon the nature of the true self. Not only is it pure bliss it is also pure consciousness. Therefore the ultimate reality, the Brahman, is not only pure bliss, but pure consciousness. With the exception of the attribute of bliss, upon which Hegel lays little stress, the account of the Brahman given in the Upanishads might serve very well for an introduction to Hegel's Absolute.

Bhagavad Gita.—The *Bhagavad Gita* composed during the eight hundred years between 600 B.C. to A.D. 200 is considerably later than the Upanishads. Although it incorporates the same basic doctrines, its statement of them is at once less clear and less uncompromising. Unlike the Upanishads, it contains elements both of pluralism and of pantheism. God in the *Gita* is both immanent and transcendent, both one and many. In fact, the *Gita* contains pantheism and deism, monism and pluralism, blended together in an inextricable confusion.

The Doctrine of Maya.—The above constitutes a brief account of the main course and conclusions of Indian philosophy. It remains to add a few words in elucidation of two distinctive doctrines which are the corner stones of the main structure. These, the doctrines of Maya and of Karma, are at once peculiar and common to Indian philosophy. Both doctrines are susceptible of a number of interpretations, and what follows, non-committal as I have tried to make it and refraining, as it does, from touching more than the fringes of the issues involved, cannot, I am fully aware, fail to seem to many controversial and to some misleading.

The purpose of the doctrine of Maya and the complementary doctrine of Avidya is to establish the status of the world of appearance. If reality is a single, non-temporal, non-substantial, spiritual unity, if it is an Absolute, "eternally accomplished, eternally existing," if the individual is himself in his inmost being this Absolute, the question arises, what account are we to give of the world as it appears? For the world as it appears is a collection of temporal, material objects, extended in space and of apparently separate individual minds which perceive them. This appearance must, one would think, if reality is a spiritual unity, be illusory. Hence arises the concept of Avidya which denotes the misperception of things as the ordinary mind misperceives them, the perception of them, that is to say, not as they are, but as they are not! Avidya, then, is a form of knowing, and Maya is the illusory appearance of the real world, as the real world appears to Avidya.

Sankaracharya, commonly known as Sankara (A.D. 789-820), the greatest of the Indian philosophers, gives cogent reasons why the world as it appears cannot be the real world, why, in fact, it must be Maya. Many of these reasons do not differ substantially from those adduced by Western philosophers, by Plato in Greece, by Hegel in Germany, and by F. H. Bradley in England, for rejecting the claim of the ordinary world of everyday life to be the real world.

For example, matter is full of contradictions. That is to say, it permits contradictory statements—that it is large, that it is small, that it is cold, that it is warm—to be made about it at the same time. Matter, again, is constantly changing; but the real world, since it is eternal, must be exempt from change. Again the material world of our ordinary experience is unbounded. It extends, that is to say, indefinitely in space and time. But the real world must be a systematic whole, and a systematic whole is a completed whole. It is for reasons such as these that Sankara denies the title of full reality to the ordinary world. Does it follow, then, that the ordinary world, the world as it appears, is a pure illusion? Many have thought so, and have adduced the authority of Sankara in support of their opinion. The notion of a world which is *pure* illusion is, however, full of difficulties. Even a world of pure illusion must, for example, in some sense *be*; for if it completely were not, it could not be known. And, if it is illusion, what account are we to give of its relation to the supreme reality, the Brahman, from which, presumably, it was generated.

It is, however, highly doubtful whether this view of the ordinary world as pure illusion was, in fact, Sankara's view. A more plausible account of his doctrine of Maya seems to be the following:

The Buddhist Doctrine of Nirvana.—Sankara, a lifelong opponent of Buddhism, was particularly concerned to criticise the Buddhist doctrine of Nirvana. According to Buddhism this life is a slavery, for, so long as we live it, we are in bondage to the desires which spring up continuously and eternally in our souls. Now desire or craving is painful, and, driven by the spur of its pain, we are led continually to take action with the object of satisfying the desire. But this action, Buddhism held, is bound to be unsuccessful. Happiness, then, can only be found in emancipation from desire. This state of emancipation is attained only after the soul has lived through the many lives to which the obligation which it is under to liquidate its Karma[1] condemns it, and is identical with the celebrated Buddhist Nirvana. The doctrines of Buddhism are thus highly pessimistic in regard to the process and prospects of living. The process they regard as necessarily unpleasant—a bad bargain in which the debit side of pain is bound to exceed the credit side of pleasure—the prospects as necessarily unsatisfying. Buddhist doctrines are also pessimistic in regard to the end of the process, which, as critics have pointed out, is scarcely, if at all, distinguishable from sheer nothingness.

Sankara severely criticised this doctrine. Life in this world, he maintained, is not necessarily a bondage and, if it is not, the reasons which Buddhists adduce against living it to the full extent of our faculties are invalid. Grant that life in this world is a mystery, nevertheless, said Sankara, we must live it. We must participate in the mystery, for we have no alternative. It was at this point in his argument that he invoked the doctrine of Maya, interpreting it to mean that the nature of this world

[1] For an account of Karma see below, pp. 53-55.

is in some sense a mystery, as opposed to the Buddhist view that it is an illusion. For if, as Sankara insisted, life in this world is not necessarily a bondage, the question immediately arises, what is, in fact, its nature? In regard to this question Sankara professed agnosticism. We do not, he insisted, know the nature of the world for the simple reason that we cannot fathom the relationship of this world to the Brahman or reality. And just because we *are* unable to fathom it, Sankara insists that the world must be regarded as an incomprehensible mystery or Maya. The world being Maya, we cannot, he suggests, dogmatically assert that it is of this character or of that, and, in particular, we are not justified in pronouncing it, with the Buddhists, a state of bondage.

The Doctrine of Karma.—The doctrine of Karma is sometimes interpreted as if it were a denial of human freedom, and an assertion of the changelessness of human destiny. The validity of this interpretation is, however, usually denied. Rightly understood, it is said, the doctrine of Karma does not deny freedom. Karma is in essence an assertion about the nature and machinery of the universe. What it asserts is that the universe is governed by a moral law. The moral law requires that all wrong-doing must be compensated, compensated by suffering on the part of the wrong-doer. Thus, when we suffer, our suffering is never entirely pointless. For it is suffering which we have brought upon ourselves by previous wrong-doing, for which we are required to compensate. The wrong-doing in question may have been, usually has been, performed in a previous life, and according to some forms of the doctrine, the status which the individual assumes in any particular life is determined by the nature and amount of the wrong-doing in previous lives for which in his present life he is required to compensate. The extent to which he will in fact compensate is a matter for his own determination and within his own control. Thus, although we are influenced by the force of Karma, we are nevertheless free ourselves to mould that force, free, that is to say, to make our Karma for the future. Such, it is asserted, is the doctrine in its true form. Ultimately a man may liquidate his past Karma, and no more Karma being generated, break the chain of birth and rebirth which the potency of past Karma entails.

But whence, one may ask, is to be derived the will-power which is necessary to enable one to adhere to the right way of life, by following which alone one is relieved from the necessity of adding new links to the chain of Karma? If a man is free, free *before* he has liquidated his Karma, well and good; there is no difficulty and he can at any moment begin the new life which the Indian sage enjoins. But how, then, we are tempted to ask, represent him as at the same time determined by the fruits of past Karma which he is reaping? We do not know; and the human mind, falling back before the mystery, has taken the line of least resistance and interpreted Karma in a sense increasingly fatalistic. This fatalistic interpretation of the doctrine has, most observers are agreed, played a considerable part in producing the mental and moral inertia which the Western mind is apt rightly or wrongly to discern in the Hindu. A pessimistic view of life and of the chances of happiness in life, a disinclination for effort, a passive resignation to curable evils—all these have been attributed by the West to the disabling effects of the doctrine of Karma, the philosophical embodiment of the native fatalism of the East. It is not for a Western writer to say how far this attribution of responsibility is justified, or how far the alleged inertia upon which it is based is, indeed, a fact.

Estimate of Indian Philosophy.—Nor is this the place to attempt any serious estimate of the value of Indian philosophy as a whole. For the reasons already given, Indian philosophy tends to be uncongenial to European philosophers, who are, indeed, apt to be quite surprisingly ignorant of its doctrines. It is, moreover, as we have seen, presented in what the Westerner finds an unattractive form. It is turgid and prolix in statement, prone to a certain lushness of metaphor and simile, and only too often suggests that Indian thinkers are under the impression that the process of stating a doctrine in different ways and with varying but, in general, increasing degrees of eloquence, makes it in some undefined manner more true. Finally, Indian philosophy is dreadfully obscure, and the Western reader can never rid himself of the suspicion that at times it mistakes obscurity for profundity. Equally, however, he cannot but suspect that underlying the obscurity there are to be found aspects of truth which the Western mind has missed, either through inadvertence or through congenital incapacity to see them, while those who are familiar with the philosophy of the West cannot avoid being struck by the frequency with which what they have been taught to regard as the latest novelties of twentieth century thinking, turn up casually, as it were, and as matters taken for granted, in this great body of speculative thought built up by the discipline of a tradition which has lasted continuously for well over two thousand years. The discovery cannot fail to sober, even to humiliate. At any rate it justifies the present writer in hazarding the view that Indian philosophy has not yet received from Western thinkers the attention to which its intrinsic merits entitle it.

Later Developments.—The Upanishads and the Sutras constitute the main corpus of Indian philosophy. From 500 to 250 B.C. the predominant philosophy was that of Buddhism. The revival of Brahminism soon after the death of Asoka in 237-6 B.C. brought in its train a number of new interpreters of the Vedas and the Upanishads in the light of the ideas both critical and constructive which had been put forward by the Buddhist school. It was to this revived Hindu school that Sankaracharya, who was considerably the most important of the individual philosophers of India, belonged.

During the Middle Ages Hindu thought came into conflict with the ideas of Islam. In India the clash between these two opposing systems resulted in the predominance of the native culture and Islamic thought was largely absorbed in Hinduism. In the eighteenth century the arrival of the Christian powers in India presented Hinduism with new problems, and a movement known as the Brahmo Samaj movement[1] arose about 1830 which sought to incorporate some of the doctrines of Christianity into the general structure of Hindu philosophy.

Hinduism is to-day again undergoing a process of criticism and challenge. The younger thinkers of contemporary India are subjecting the traditional tenets of Hindu philosophy to severe and continuous critical examination. How many of the classical doctrines will survive this contemporary criticism it is as yet too early to say.

[1] See for an account of this, Chapter VI, pp. 139-141.

CHAPTER III

THE SEARCH FOR BEAUTY

§ 1. General Character of Indian Art

The Impulses that Lead Men to Create.—The impulses which lead men to produce what is called art are, broadly speaking, three in number. There is, first, the impulse to make beautiful things or beautiful sounds. There is, secondly, the impulse to copy or to reproduce the things and sounds of this world—landscapes and the faces and figures of people, the crowing of cocks, the murmuring of brooks and the clamour of storms. There is, thirdly, the impulse to render or to express certain feelings experienced by the artist which he believes to be valuable or important, and which he wishes to communicate to others by making of them a concrete and permanent record. And since, inevitably, feelings call up that which has aroused or evoked them, the inspiration of this third kind of art derives from the impulse to make a commemorative witness to some beautiful or holy thing which has inspired awe or reverence in the artist no less than from the impulse to express the feelings which the beautiful or holy thing has aroused.

The first kind of art may be called formal; the artist's purpose is to make a certain form or pattern of shapes, colours, or sounds, which possesses beauty, or, as some prefer to say, significance in its own right; the second, representative, the purpose being to make a copy or representation of things which already exist: the third, expressive, the purpose being to express something which the artist has felt. I do not wish to suggest that these impulses exist or operate in isolation or that any one of them is normally the exclusive source of any single work of creative art. On the contrary, all three may be present in the inspiration of a particular work—for example, the second movement of Beethoven's Sixth Symphony may be regarded as the outcome (i) of the composer's desire to weave a beautiful pattern of sound—to make, in short, something which is lovely in itself—(ii) of his desire to imitate, albeit casually and by way of a diversion, the sounds of the farmyard, and, more seriously, to produce sounds which recall the fury and the majesty of a storm, and (iii) of his desire to express the feelings aroused in him by pastoral scenes, and the calms that follow storms. Nevertheless, it is the case that most art is predominantly inspired by one or other of these three impulses, and has as its primary object the achievement of one or other of these three ends—namely, the creation of beautiful shapes or sounds, the representation of already existing objects and sounds, or the expression of feelings. Thus English pictorial art in the nineteenth century was predominantly representational; German music in the eighteenth century was predominantly formal; and Indian art in all ages is predominantly expressive.

Characteristics of Formal Art.—It is this circumstance which distinguishes Indian art most sharply from the art of the West. Most European artists have either sought to render people and things—have either, that is to say, been portrait or landscape painters—or have tried to make objects or collections of objects that possessed formal beauty. Now the landscape or the portrait is primarily representative. It must from its very nature be a picture *of* something. Pictures of still life, as, for example, when an orange, a flask of wine and a crust of bread are portrayed disposed upon a table, are less representative and more formal, but they still represent. Pictures which consist solely of arrangements of lines and colours and shapes are almost entirely formal. Their *raison d'être* is the creation of beautiful or significant combinations. Chinese artists, for example, were primarily concerned with the formal qualities of the work which they produced. While their art is admittedly in part the expression of feeling, its primary purpose is the evocation of beauty. You see a clay pot or a china vase, and you are thrilled by its significance. Why you are thrilled you cannot say—at least, you cannot unless you are a philosopher, when you evolve a metaphysical theory to explain the peculiar quality of the emotion you feel. But the mysterious thrill which you obtain from the perception of the intrinsic qualities and formal relations of the lines and curves and colours of the piece of pottery is the source of your appreciation of the work of art and of the value which you attribute to it. You do not think of the artist; you do not ask yourself what is the meaning which he may be wishing to convey, and you do not try yourself to feel the emotions he may be seeking to express. The pot or vase is its own justification and its own *raison d'être*; it means nothing and it symbolises nothing.

Indian Art.—I cannot more summarily convey what is the peculiar and distinguishing quality of Indian art than by saying that these precisely are the questions and considerations which it *does* provoke. What, you wonder, is the meaning which the artist is seeking to convey; what the emotions which his work expresses? Who or what, however imperfectly apprehended, has aroused these emotions? What, in other words, does the work of art symbolise? For obviously it is not, it cannot be its own justification; emphatically it does not contain within itself its own *raison d'être*. Always and insistently it points the spectator to something behind and beyond itself. It is at once a medium for some emotion the artist has felt and which, by the device of expressing the emotion in the medium, he seeks to make you feel too, and a clue to that which has aroused it. Thus Indian art rarely—if I may be pardoned the expression—stands on its own feet, as art: it performs the office of handmaid to some purpose beyond itself.

Now this something is reality,[1] and the purpose is the expression of the artist's apprehension of reality. This is not, of course, to deny that the Indian artists both created beautiful things and

[1] See Chapter II, pp. 27, 28 and 45-49, for an explanation of the peculiar significance of this word in Indian thought.

valued them because they were beautiful. Even if the artist had not been interested in beauty, the circumstances in which he created and which were the occasion of his creating, would have ensured at least the effort to produce it. For in India, as elsewhere, art was under the wing of patronage, and the artist produced at the behest of some great man or king who engaged and encouraged him. The monarchs of India employed artists to construct their public buildings and to beautify their palaces, and priests employed artists to decorate their temples, when they did not decorate them themselves. Thus the incentive to create beauty was always present, even if it owned no higher source than the desire to please a patron. But, though present, it was subsidiary ; for, though the occasion of the artist's production may have been an order from the emperor for the decoration of his palace, the designing of its gardens or the frescoing of its walls, its purpose was nearly always the glorification of God. When the artist's work was the decoration of a temple or the building of a shrine, the two aims, the evocation of beauty and the glorification of God, coalesced. One produced works of beauty *in order to* glorify God, or—to translate into the language which I have been using—the impulse to create a beautiful thing and the impulse to express the feelings of veneration and awe evoked by the mysteries of one's religion, operated together so that the endeavours of the sculptor or painter drew their inspiration from two motives which had harmoniously blended to become one.

Its Religious Motive.—For the feelings of whose expression the Indian artist sought to make stone and paint the medium, were usually, in some periods they were exclusively, religious. Intensely sensitive, the Indian artist was at once conscious of the spiritual reality which underlay the world of sense and animated by feelings of reverence for that which his spiritual insight revealed to him. His art he used both as a method of communicating these feelings and as a symbol of the reality which aroused them. You cannot, it may be said, describe God in words; nor can you in the language of everyday life convey your conception of the innermost reality of the universe. But you may be able to do these things in art. Art, in fact, is the window through which men may gaze upon reality.

It is on these lines that I would give meaning to the common but ambiguous expression, that Indian artists used art as a means of conveying spiritual truths. What were these truths ? We have already glanced at them in our survey of Indian philosophy. Briefly they were that the world of which our senses make us aware is in the last resort illusory, that reality is One, that God is spirit, and that by practising a particular psychological technique the human soul can become conscious of its oneness with this spirit. In so far as he employs his art as a means of conveying certain conceptions in regard to the nature of the universe, and in particular *these* conceptions, the Indian artist is a philosopher first and an artist second. He creates things of undeniable beauty, but their beauty is ancillary to his main purpose—

the expression of spiritual truth. The period in European art with which Indian art has the closest kinship, is, therefore, that of the Middle Ages, when, by the building of cathedrals, the decoration of churches, the illumination of manuscripts, and the composition of masses and chorales, artists and craftsmen sought at once to glorify God and to convey their conception of God.

Anonymity of Indian Art.—A further parallel is afforded by the anonymity of the artists. The names of the architects of St. Sophia at Constantinople and of the lovely Byzantine sixth century churches are unknown to us. The builders of the churches and cathedrals of the Middle Ages are anonymous and so, too, are the great Byzantine primitives, those, for example, who set their mosaics at Ravenna. And, broadly speaking, we do not know the names of the artists of India. It was, indeed, of a piece with the Indian tradition that no painter or sculptor should sign his name. If you paint in order to express your personality, it is a matter of supreme moment that your personality should be expressed, expressed and recognised. Hence you sign your picture. But if your art is merely the vehicle of a religious impulse, the medium of a message which transcends you, your personal identity is a matter of supreme unimportance. For the artist inspired by his God is, in his own regard, little more than a fountain pen through which flows the stream of religious inspiration. And just as what the fountain pen writes is dictated not by it but for it, so the man who conceives himself to be the vehicle of an impulse from a spiritual but unseen reality, cannot, except in a purely formal sense, be regarded as personally responsible for the character which his art assumes.

Indian art, then, is for the most part anonymous, and it is anonymous because it is a byproduct of Indian religion. There are, of course, exceptions to this generalisation. For a period of several centuries after A.D. 1000 pictures and mosaics appear which bear the signatures of their artists. But during this period the Moguls were ruling India, and the Moguls, as we shall shortly see, introduced Persian influences into Indian art. Under these influences painters were willing for a time to devote their skill to the making of vivid representations of people and things. But this period of the Moguls represented a departure from the main tradition of Indian art, to which in later times artists returned. With these preliminary observations we may proceed to give a brief chronological sketch of some of the main developments of Indian art.

§2. The History of Indian Art

Continuity of Indian Art.—Indian works of art take for the most part the form of shrines, temples and monuments. Some of these are still extant. Others have been laid bare by the recent work of excavators. The earliest works of this type are certain antiquities recently discovered at Mohenjo Daro in the Indus valley. They include limestone figures of bearded men, terra-cotta figures of animals and a blue tablet with pictographic characters representing a cross-legged figure with worshippers kneeling on his right and left. The figures on this tablet bear a striking resemblance to those which become familiar in Buddhist art of the historical period (*circa* 400 to 200 B.C.). These early antiques, dating from the period of Indian pre-history, have in general two very striking affinities. The first is with the remains which have been found on Sumerian sites in Mesopotamia which are dated somewhere between the fifth and the third millennium B.C. This affinity confirms the suggestion already made [1] that the early culture of India was continuous with or a development of the still earlier culture of Mesopotamia. The second affinity is with works of Indian art which date from a much later period (probably from somewhere between 1000 and 400 B.C.) found at Taxilla and Pataliputra in Behar, at a considerable distance from the Indus valley. This affinity suggests a continuity of tradition in Indian art extending from pre-historical to historical times, a continuity which, as we shall subsequently have occasion to note, runs unbroken from the earliest period through the Middle Ages and into the contemporary world.

Vedic Art.—Of art in the Vedic period we have very few records. The Vedic Aryans seem to have been proficient in carpentry, house-building and chariot construction, but the arts of painting and sculpture which flourished in later periods appear to have been unknown to them. Decoration was, however, widely practised, the articles of house-

[1] See Chapter I, p. 1.

hold use which have survived from this period being nearly all decorated in some way. The decorations are symbolical rather than representative; that is to say, they indicate ideal aspirations and embody abstract conceptions; they do not represent concrete things. In this respect they foreshadow later Indian art, which, as I have already pointed out, is essentially symbolical. Some, indeed, have deduced from the fact that later Indian art retains the symbolical character which first appears in the decoration of these Vedic household utensils that later artists were consciously influenced by the Vedic tradition, and they have argued that this early work must have had a greater artistic value than the specimens which have come down to us would appear at first sight to suggest.

The historical period of Indian art may be said to have begun in the first half of the sixth century B.C. The later Vedic books mention storied buildings, cups and spoons of gold and silver, musical instruments, thrones and jewellery. In the Jatakas or legends[1] (*circa* 600 B.C. to A.D. 300) we come across the actual names of goldsmiths and craftsmen. Extant remains are, however, exceedingly few.

Period of Maurya Art: 320 to 185 B.C.—By the time of Asoka Indian art had already reached a high level of development. Such examples of the art of the period as have survived are mainly architectural. Among the most notable are the monolithic rail at Sarnath, the altar rail at Bodgaya, a pillar covered with inscriptions at Mathura, various Buddhist

[1] See Chapter IV, pp. 92, 93, for an account of these.

chapter houses known as Caitya-halls at Sanchi and Sonari and the excavated Caitya-halls or chapter houses in the Barabar hills in Behar. Asoka's Palace at Pataliputra, which was still intact in the fifth century A.D., was highly praised by Fa Hien, the Chinese pilgrim, but no traces of it now remain. A number of interesting sculptures of the late Maurya period (*circa* 200 B.C.) have also been found at Sarnath. They show the existence of a well-developed style of sculpture and a high level of technical accomplishment. Other fragments of this period are some bas-reliefs showing moving figures found at Sarnath. These show great executant ability and a considerable feeling for the rhythm of movement. Groups of highly stylised Maurya terra-cotta figures have been found in Pataliputra and Taxilla.

The differences in character between the remains of this period found in various parts of the country suggest that they are the work of several different schools of artists.

Sunga, Andhra, Indo-Parthian and Kusana Periods: 200 B.C. to A.D. 320.—After the fall of the Maurya Empire, extant examples of Indian artistic work in stone become much more numerous. The period of five hundred years which elapsed between the fall of the Mauryas and the rise of the Guptas witnessed the domination of the Sungas, a Hindu dynasty, in the north, and of the Andhras, a Dravidian dynasty in the south. The north-west was ruled by a series of Indo-Parthian monarchs. As may be expected, therefore, this period furnishes examples of many different schools and styles of art.

Monuments and temples are its most characteristic products. The most famous monuments are the Bharhut (Nagodh State) and Sanci (Bhopal State) Stúpas or burial mounds and their railings and gateways. Stupas, a word which originally meant funeral mounds, is the name later given to any shrine containing a relic of the Buddha. The Bharhut brick Stupa probably dates from about 150 B.C. and belongs to the Sunga period. Images of Devatas (gods) are inscribed on the gate posts and exquisite groups of floral, animal and monster figures are represented on the railing medallions and copings. Both at Bharhut and Sanci floral designs are treated with an unerring sense of decorative values.

In the south there have recently been excavated at Amaravati a number of Stupas, which are dated about A.D. 200. The workmanship of the statues, altar rails, columns and so on which adorn the Stupas is closely related both in regard to style and form to that of the similar work at Bharhut and Sanci in the north, although the Amaravati work is somewhat more formal and elaborate. The art of this period is, however, chiefly differentiated from earlier and subsequent Indian art by reason of the fact that it is not essentially religious. Art, that is to say, is not during the period of 500 years between the Maurya and the Gupta Empires treated as a means of glorifying God or of expressing the religious aspirations of man ; artists seem to have been concerned mainly or even solely with the creation of beauty. Let a decoration be beautiful in and for itself, and the purpose of him who made it was fulfilled. Thus the characteristic qualities of the art of this period are realistic and sensuous. Artists, in other words, represented creatures and things, concentrated upon the appeal of creatures and things to the visual sense, and endeavoured to enhance that appeal in the representations they made of them. I do not mean to suggest by this that the Buddhist artists did not use painting and decoration as a pictorial medium for narrating the history and legends of the Buddhist faith. They did, in fact, do so. All that I wish to convey is that the *primary* purpose of this art is not religious but æsthetic. The artist, in fact, although choosing religious subjects is preoccupied rather with the formal significance of his work than with its effect in expressing or arousing religious emotion.

The above constitutes a brief historical sketch of the main trends of Indian art down to the end of the third century A.D. We shall now proceed to comment upon some of its distinctive features. For this purpose it will be convenient to treat the various arts separately.

Sculpture.—Before the time of Asoka the principal arts of India were those of weaving, wood-carving, various kinds of metal work and certain types of painting. The craft of the mason and the stone-carver was practised comparatively rarely. Wood was plentiful and was as a consequence generally preferred to stone for structural and decorative purposes. The art of wood-carving was, indeed, highly developed, and the early craftsmen who worked in wood may justly be regarded as the forerunners of Indian sculpture. The carving of the rails of the shrines at Bharhut and the sculptures at

Amaravati, for example, definitely suggest that the sculptor was reproducing in stone wooden prototypes. The technique used by these sculptors is, in fact, simply the technique of the wood-worker and metal-worker transferred to stone.

When Asoka became emperor, he employed the energies of his subjects in the construction of large numbers of magnificent public works. The majority of these were memorials and shrines; in fact, legend credits Asoka with the creation of no less than eighty-four thousand shrines. Asoka was favourably disposed towards all the arts, and under his patronage there was a great burst of artistic activity. Buddhism had become the State religion, and Buddhist priests sought in works of art at once to express their faith and to symbolise its meaning. Thus, wherever a monument was erected or a shrine built, there grew up a prominent art centre which presently began to develop a school of its own. The modes of working elaborated at the various schools of this period rapidly acquired the status of traditional techniques which were handed on from one generation of masons and craftsmen to another. Thus, even as late as the Amaravati period (*circa* A.D. 100) we find that the processes and techniques of the Indian artists are still indistinguishable from those of the days of Asoka.

Asoka's proselytising efforts were not continued by his immediate successors, and as a result the source of inspiration which flowed from the impulse to spread the Buddhist faith by pictorial decoration and sculpture dried up.

Gandhara School: 140 B.C. to A.D. 320.—In the meantime, however, on the North-western frontier of India, the Indo-Bactrian school of Gandhara had arisen. Gandhara was a country in which stone suitable for building and sculpture was actually more plentiful than wood. The Gandhara artists, therefore, began from the outset to use stone as a medium for the expression of their artistic impulse. Moreover Gandhara, situated, as it was, on the North-west frontier, was closer than the rest of India to the outlying parts of the Roman Empire and was, therefore, more susceptible to Greco-Roman influences than Eastern and Southern India.

There is current controversy as to the extent to which Greco-Roman conceptions influenced Indian art as a whole, both during this period and during that immediately ensuing. The most widely supported view seems to be that the Gandhara period of Indian art was a purely transitional one and that, although traces of Greco-Roman influence are undoubtedly noticeable even in the Amaravati sculptures, the work of the Gandhara School is in no sense representative of the typical Indian sculptural technique and does not express the typical Indian ideals of divinity.

The great cultural centres of India at this time were the Indian universities of Taxilla, Benares, Sridhanya-Kataka on the banks of the Krishna and the famous university of Nalanda. Art and sculpture were officially studied at the universities, and the influence of the university art schools was more or less supreme throughout the country. In comparison with this influence, which was of purely Indian origin, that of Hellenism is unimportant. It is to the direct teaching of these great educational centres rather than to the occasional intrusion of Persian and European influences and techniques that we must look for an explanation of the development of Indian art, the fact of the matter being that India was not, during the period of the Gandhara school, dependent for its sculpture and ideas on any other country. On the contrary, it was India that influenced the other peoples of Asia, either directly by her own teaching or indirectly by her example. In so far as India made use of western ideas, she did so only to transform them, transmuting by the subtle alchemy of her own culture what in the process of transmutation was also enriched. Thus while the Hellenistic element both in modelling and in image-making frequently enters into the work of Indian artists, it enriches, but never dominates the national style. It was in the work of the Gandharan school that this foreign influence was most prominent. In the sculptures at Amaravati in Southern India we see Indian art passing from the naturalistic modes of the Asokan epoch into the idealistic style which is distinctive of later Indian art and which became the medium of its highest expression.

The Gupta Period: A.D. 320 to 600.—Under the Guptas, Indian sculpture developed the full potentialities of the distinctively Indian style. The Gupta period, in fact, constitutes the culmination of all that had gone before. In the north-west the Gandhara school continued to flourish, although in an increasingly Indianised form; but the achievements of the Gandhara artists are of small importance in comparison with those of the Gupta school. Three characteristics of this school may be noticed. There is, first, a great prevalence of images and statues. In the previous period the making of images and statues had been still a comparatively new art, and statues had, therefore, accorded to them an outstanding and often an isolated position. Magnificent images of the Buddha were constructed, but no attempt was made to fit them into their environment. Considered in and by themselves they were highly impressive, but they were not elements in an artistic whole. During the Gupta period images and statues were designed to form an integral part of a pattern that transcended them. From this pattern they could not be removed without destroying both their own effect and that of the larger whole to which they belonged.

In the second place, art under the Guptas is used deliberately as a language. It is used, that is to say, to express something which the artist feels and to communicate that feeling to those who contemplate his works. Now this feeling which art is used to express and communicate is primarily religious. Art, in other words, becomes a medium for the statement of spiritual conceptions. While this generalisation is primarily suggested by a consideration of Gupta sculpture, the truth which it embodies applies equally to painting, dancing and the other fine arts of the period. In the third place, whether because of the function it performed as a medium for the expression of religious feeling, or in virtue of æsthetic considerations of which ultimately no account can be given, the art of the Gupta period is beautiful. In the last resort beauty is unanalysable and indefinable. Its essence and its nature elude statement in words. People have, however, sought to describe the peculiar feelings which the Indian art of this period has produced in them by saying that it is serene, that it is energetic, that it is spiritual, and that it is voluptuous. These characteristics seem, no doubt, to be in part contradictory. It is, nevertheless, the fact that all are not only attributed to Gupta art in general, but to the same particular work of art. I say "Gupta art", but I might with equal justice have written "Indian art of all periods", since the work of the Gupta period came in due course to be regarded in the light of a model by the artists of later periods. Just as the Gupta style unified all past and existing styles and brought them to their fullest development, so it served as a model for all future styles and came to stand for the national artistic ideal.

Some of the most outstanding examples of the sculpture of this great period are, (1) the statues of Buddha belonging to what is known as the Mathura school, one of which, a magnificent standing Buddha, has been lately found at Jamalpur. (2) The well-known seated Buddha from Sarnath. (3) Buddha figures in relief at Ajanta. (4) Buddha figures on the façades at Karli. (5) A Bodhisattva[1] torso from Sanci, now to be seen in the Victoria and Albert Museum.

[1] A Bodhisattva is an early incarnation of Buddha, see Chapter IV, p. 92, for a further account.

Besides stone work there are extant some wonderful examples of metal work belonging to the Gupta period, of which the colossal image from Sultanganj is perhaps the most famous.

Architecture.—As we shall have occasion in a later chapter to point out,[1] the village in ancient India was a highly organised social community; it was in village communities that the great bulk of the people in early Buddhist times lived. At a very early period the Indians of the villages appear to have developed an architectural sense, and their calculations and instructions for building and planning houses, roads and villages are embodied in the Sanskrit book entitled *Manasara Silpa-Sastra.*

The Silpa-Sastras.—These instructions are characteristically imbued throughout with a moral and, religious purpose. They insist, for example, upon the high level of intellectual and moral culture which is necessary for a master builder or Sthapati.

Problems of town and village planning are also dealt with in great detail in the Silpa-Sastras. Although architecture is approached from a symbolical point of view, yet the subject is treated with scientific exactness, marked common sense, and continuous reference to the sanitary and military needs of the community. This combination of the religious and the utilitarian is particularly Indian; it is almost as if even the drains were planned to the glory of God. Almost but not quite, for there were no drains.

The urge to create beautiful buildings and temples which received its impetus from the patronage of

[1] See Chapter V, pp. 119-122.

Asoka, did not remain satisfied with the building of plain houses and villages. For hundreds of years the village *Sthapati* or master builders, who have come to be regarded as the founders of the architecture of India, experimented with a number of architectural styles. The developments of Indian architecture for which these village builders were responsible culminated in the achievements of the Gupta period. The number of Stupas (burial mounds), Viharas (monasteries), Caitya-halls (chapter houses), and Sikhara (shrines) surviving from this period (A.D. 320 to 600) bear witness not only to the fertility but also to the artistic integrity of these villagers. The well-known Dhamekh Stupa at Sarnath, the Viharas at Ajanta, and the Durga temple of Aihole are some of the outstanding examples of their art.

Indo-Saracenic Renaissance.—After the Mohammedan conquest the arts of sculpture and architecture disappeared from large parts of India. This period of comparative artistic extinction lasted until the eleventh and twelfth centuries A.D. There then occurred a revival known as the Indo-Saracenic Renaissance. As a result of contact and conflict with Islamic civilisation, Indian constructional art in the Middle Ages flowered anew. A particular development of architectural and constructional activity for which the period is famous is the planning and designing of gardens. The Taj Mahal, which belongs to this period, is one of the many fruits of the happy marriage of India and Islam, the Islamic influence being seen in the exuberant decoration with which this lovely building is enriched.

When Hindu builders and craftsmen built palaces and designed gardens for their Mogul masters, they did not abandon their own traditions. Inevitably, they introduced their own ideas into the patterns of Mohammedan architecture which under Indian influence became insensibly transformed, until it too served to symbolise religious conceptions and to express human aspirations. The Taj Mahal, for example, in spite of its profuse decoration, is a highly symbolical building and the same may be said of other Mogul buildings at Fatepur-Sikri and Agra.

There has been in recent times a movement to revive the Indian tradition in architecture and, in spite of the influence of Europe, the native Indian style of architecture is slowly gaining ground. Thus the new capital of India at Delhi, although planned and supervised by English officials, has an Indian appearance, with typical Indian decorations, façades, and frontage.

Painting.—Broadly speaking, Indian paintings may be divided into four main groups, each of which is representative of a different style—namely the Hindu, the Buddhist, the Rajput or Mogul and the modern.

Hindu Painting. Prehistoric Vedic and Buddhist Primitives, circa 800 B.C. to A.D.—There is little evidence of painting in prehistoric and Vedic times. Such pictorial remains as have survived are to be found on the walls of a group of caves in Central India, which are covered with primitive and crudely drawn records of hunting scenes. Isolated cave drawings are found in many parts of India. There is, furthermore, some evidence that many of the rock-cut buildings, ascribed to pre-Buddhist times, were originally adorned with frescoes which have been destroyed by the action of sun and rain. Finally, there are numerous references in the literature of the time which suggest that before and during the early Buddhist period painting in India was already a well-known and highly developed art. These references are particularly frequent in the *Vinaya Pithaka*, a Pali Buddhist work, which was probably written in the third or fourth century B.C., by which time it appears that the art of painting was being widely practised. It cannot be said, however, that the examples of the period which survive indicate a very high quality of artistry.

Buddhist Period of Painting: A.D. to 700.—The great age of Indian painting, known as the Buddhist, dawned about the beginning of the Christian era. Unfortunately the examples which survive are very few. Pre-eminent are the frescoes in the rock-cut temples of Ajanta. The particular interest of these frescoes lies in the fact that they constitute a record of the gradual development of the art of painting in India over a span of some six hundred years. Some date from the very earliest period of the Buddhist school; others, painted some six hundred years later, are the products of its maturity. Other notable remains are the friezes at Sigirya in Ceylon and the wall paintings of Bagh. These latter, which date from the period of Buddhist maturity (fifth century A.D.), are very numerous and indicate an exuberant activity as well as a high level of technical accomplishment. Their purpose is to illustrate by pictorial parables the truths of the Buddhist religion. They are, therefore, in the strict sense of the word, expressionist, the artists who painted them being obviously motivated by a desire to express the feelings of devotion and reverence which their religion inspired. These Buddhist wall paintings are, therefore, concerned at once to illustrate and to glorify the religion that excited their authors. Modern scholars believe that the paintings of this period were exceedingly numerous. The language of art was for the Buddhist devotee the most natural vehicle for the expression and communication of his feelings, and, as Buddhism spread, painting was increasingly used as an adjunct to the missionary work of Buddhist proselytisers. The period was, moreover, one which broadly corresponded with the golden age of the Guptas. The Gupta Empire, as we have seen,[1] gave India several centuries of peace, and the freedom from wars and violence in which artists lived may be supposed to have encouraged not only artistic production in general but, in particular, the form of art which was an instrument of religion.

The Rajput or Mogul School: A.D. 1550 to 1900.—From the eighth to the sixteenth centuries there is little evidence of any creative painting in India. After the fall of the Gupta Empire, Buddhism declined. With the decline of Buddhism, painting diminished in importance and the plastic arts took pride of place. There are still extant some exquisitely illuminated book illustrations surviving from this

[1] See Chapter I, pp. 9, 10.

period, but throughout the major part of India during the eight hundred years that intervened between the fall of the Guptas and the coming of the Moguls painting seems to have been little practised.

It was in the Rajput States of Central India that the tradition of Indian painting was chiefly preserved during the years of confusion which followed the break-up of the Gupta Empire. Painters found favour in the courts of the numerous small Hindu kings between whom Central India was divided, and when the Mogul dynasty had firmly established itself and had energy and leisure to spare for the patronage of the arts and crafts, the artists who had survived and continued to practise their art in the courts of these petty Central Indian States gradually began to flock to the court of the Great Mogul.

Styles of Rajput Painting.—Rajput painting may be divided into two main styles known as Kalms. There is, first, the Jeypore Kalm. This derives its name from Jeypore, one of the leading Rajput States, which had given shelter to a number of artists who there developed a distinctive school or style of painting. The other Kalm is the Kangra, which derived its name from a group of small States in the Punjab Himalayas, of which Kangra was the chief. The Kangra group also developed a special style of its own.

The Rajput painters might more accurately be described as craftsmen than as artists in the strict sense of the word "artist". During the Buddhist period the painting and construction of temples and shrines had been largely undertaken by Buddhist priests, and their work reflected the exclusiveness of their faith, their learning and their class. Its distinguishing characteristic is remoteness from ordinary life. Little attempt is made to represent natural objects or to reproduce the human form. Buddhist art, in fact, gives the impression of being concerned not with this world but with the next. But the Rajput painters had no such religious intention. They were for the most part ordinary, secular men who happened to be skilled in the craft of painting, and, like the great Dutch painters were moved to record the scenes of their daily lives. In the work of the Rajput artists, therefore, we find for the first time in the history of Indian painting pictures of the domestic life and day to day activities of ordinary men and women. When the Rajput painters began to gather at the courts of the Great Moguls, this secular tendency was further developed. The religious and symbolic tradition which had been to some extent carried on by the Rajput painters was now abandoned. The spirit was forgotten and the flesh came into its own. Thus the exquisite miniatures for which the Mogul period is famous are for the most part actual portraits of living people. The spirit, no doubt, still exerts its claims; the portraits are never *mere* photographs. It is the innermost character, no less than the facial contours of the sitter, that is revealed to the eye of the spectator. But the same may be said of the best miniature work of any age and country, and the Rajput, although by no means the least attractive, is certainly the least distinctive of the schools of Indian painting.

Modern School: A.D. 1760 to 1936.—With the fall of the Mogul Empire and the outbreak of civil war among the various states into which it broke up, painting in India again decayed. Miniature portraiture was still practised in some of the centres of Mogul influence, but the examples that survive show a marked falling off in quality.

It was not until the last decade of the nineteenth century that an æsthetic revival began, and a small group of Bengali painters, led by Abanindranath Tagore, bore witness to the stirring of a new inspiration in Indian art. The influence of this school is now spreading to all parts of India. The work of these modern artists constitutes a return to the ancient Indian tradition. There is no slavish imitation of historical styles, but there is an attempt to incorporate all that is most distinctive in the Indian art of the past. The spectator who looks at one of these modern pictures with a sufficiently close attention cannot fail to find in it traces of all the various influences which have gone to the making of Indian art. This great variety of style affords scope for individual originality and initiative. But when the work of the Bengali school is considered as a whole, it will be found to embody the same intention to express the mental and spiritual conceptions of the artist as has dominated Indian art during the great periods. This modern school, that is to say, is still expressive, religious and symbolic.

CHAPTER IV

THE SEARCH FOR EXPRESSION

General Character of Indian Literature.—In the previous chapter I have noted as a distinguishing characteristic of Indian art that its purpose is to communicate emotions and to convey ideas, rather than to create objects and sounds which are beautiful in themselves. Now the communication of emotions and the conveying of ideas constitute what is essentially the function of literature. For literature consists of words and the function of words is to communicate meaning.

In the chapter on Indian philosophy I drew attention to the peculiar form in which the great bulk of Indian philosophical writings have been cast. Indian philosophy, I pointed out, consists less of a series of statements by men who, starting from no preconceived standpoint, have set out to discover what is true, than of a series of commentaries by those who, already convinced that they knew where the truth was to be found, set out to explain and to interpret the sacred writings which enshrined it. Indian philosophy, in fact, savours less of a work of exploration than of an office of piety. One has not, it seems, to discover, but to elucidate what has already been discovered. The elucidation inevitably assumes the character of a critical commentary, and critical commentary falls within the province of literature.

Where art usurps the function of literature, it is to be expected that literature will be found to be the supreme art. Where philosophy subordinates speculation to scholarship, one may look to scholarship for an expression, at once the most characteristic and the most satisfactory, of the genius of the race. It is not, therefore, matter for surprise that it is in literature that Indians have chiefly excelled, and that it is to the discipline of scholarship rather than to that of science that they have with the greatest readiness submitted themselves.

Literature, indeed, is the fundamental form of the expression of Hindu creativity. Sanskrit, a language which belongs to the Indo-European group and has been the chief literary vehicle of Indian thought, is an instrument admirably adapted to give expression to every subtlety of human thought, every *nuance* of human feeling. Continuously in our survey of the various aspects of Indian civilisation, whether our immediate concern has been with religion, philosophy or art, we have found that the subject matter of our enquiry partakes more of the quality of literature than of anything else. Nobody can read Indian religious writings, for example, without being struck by the frequency with which he comes upon lines of great lyrical beauty. Thus in the following from the *Rig-Veda* :—

"We gaze upon her as she comes
The shining daughter of the sky
The mighty darkness she uncovers,
And light she makes, the pleasant one that we see."

the beauty of expression is quite recognisable even in translation. The writings of Indian poets and dramatists, historians and biographers, contain evidence not only of richness of imagination and variety of feeling, but of a remarkable talent for expressing precisely those moments of experience, for describing precisely those adventures of the spirit, which chiefly give to human life its meaning and its significance.

Indian literature may be conveniently divided into three main periods, namely the Vedic, the Gupta, and the Mediæval and Modern. These classifications are neither watertight nor exhaustive. They will, however, serve as a convenient basis for its purposes of exposition.

Vedic Literature.—The Vedas (*circa* 1000 B.C.) have always been regarded by Indian writers of successive generations as the fountain head of Indian literature. Indian scholars delight in classification, and they have divided the Vedas into the four main groups described in the first chapter.[1] After the Vedas come what are known as the Upa-Vedas, or inferior Vedas. These are also four in number, and, with the exception of the second, deal in a non-scientific manner with subjects that would now be regarded as falling within the province of science. They are (1) the *Avur-Veda*, which treats of medicine; (2) the *Gandharva-Veda*, whose subject is music and dancing; (3) the *Dhanur-Veda*, or the science of archery and military tactics; and (4) the *Sthapatya-Veda*, also known as *Silpa*, dealing with architecture.

[1] See p. 3.

Vedangas.—In addition to the Upa-Vedas, there are six auxiliary works, known as the Vedangas, dating from roughly the same period (1000 B.C.) whose study was considered to be necessary for the sacrificial system. These were: (1) *Siksha*, the science of phonetics; (2) *Chandas*, the science of metrics; (3) *Vya Karana*, the science of grammar; (4) *Nirukta*, a treatise on etymology; (5) *Jyotisha*, a treatise on astronomy; and (6) *Kalpa*, the science of ceremonial.

The Vedas, the Upa-Vedas and the Vedangas do not all possess equal literary merit. Some of them are lacking in colour; their style is purely formal and they are overloaded with a mass of boring and unimportant detail. Many of the poems on the other hand, are directly imbued with that feeling of wonder and ecstasy, which is the soul of most great poetry. The dignity and simplicity with which this wonder is expressed, more particularly in the hymns contained in the *Rig-Veda*, are such as are to be found only in works of first-rate literary importance. Some of the stories of the Vedas were amplified and dramatised by Sanskrit playwrights of a later age.

Law Literature.—The Indian literature of this early period and of the period immediately following (*circa* 1000 to 500 B.C.) was not confined to religious poems and philosophical treatises. It embraces in addition a number of works on legal subjects. Notable among these are the *Dharma-Shastras* of Baudhayana. These are regarded, not only by scholars, but by all orthodox Hindus, as laying down the fundamental pattern upon which all subsequent Hindu societies have been constructed.

The Code or Institutes of Manu, as the *Dharma-Shastras* are sometimes called, dates from several centuries before the Christian era and is divided into four parts. The first part (*a*) is called *Achara* or Immemorial Practices, the second (*b*) *Vyavahara* or Legal and Governmental Practices, the third (*c*) *Prayaschitta* or Penitential Exercises, the fourth (*d*) *Karmaphala* or The Consequences of Acts. The Code or Institutes of Manu comprises in all twelve books. Beginning with the story of creation it prescribes the whole ethical and social duty of man, and culminates in directions as to the way of life which must be followed, if we are to emancipate ourselves from the chain of births and rebirths to which Karma commits us.

Political Literature.—The next important contribution to literature, Kautilya's *Artha-Shastra*, belongs to the domain of statecraft. Discovered in 1909, by an Indian scholar called Shama Sastri, it is supposed to have been written somewhere between 500 and 400 B.C., although some scholars put the date considerably later. The *Artha-Shastra* may best be described as a dissertation on the art of ruling. It describes administrative practice, gives recommendations in regard to the details of government, and prescribes regulations for the conduct of the governed. Throughout it is characterised by a freshness and realism which suggest that the author had first-hand experience of the actual problems of which he so engagingly writes. Only the practising statesman could, one feels, have brought himself to be quite so devastatingly candid. If, as seems likely, the work is the result of first-hand experience, we may deduce with considerable assurance that the author was living in a community in which the art of government was already highly developed. The various topics which are discussed—agriculture and commerce, the relations of central and municipal governments, problems of foreign and internal policy, the attitude of government to the arts and crafts, the administration of forests and mines—are such as would arise only in a highly-developed community. So refreshingly frank and outspoken is the *Artha-Shastra*, so completely emancipated is its author from scruples, both moral and religious, and so wholeheartedly devoted to the state, whose interests he regards as paramount, that Kautilya has been called the Indian Machiavelli.

Sex and Marriage.—Another branch of this early literature takes for its province questions of sex and marriage. The first great work of this kind which has come down to us, the *Kama-Sutra* or *Kama-Shastra* of Vatsyana Mallanaga, is supposed to have been written about A.D. 300.[1] Vatsyana was a physician and his work, which he regarded as a contribution to Ayurveda, the science of medicine, is divided into seven parts in which he discusses freely and frankly the various aspects of sex life, and gives advice which has a curiously modern flavour on such subjects as how to achieve happiness in marriage. The attitude of the *Kama-Sutra* is rational, its manner forthright, and it has consider-

[1] The date is only approximate. The *Kama-Sutra* may have been composed several hundred years earlier.

able claims to be considered the first book on the subject imbued with the scientific spirit, which has come down to us. In this connection it is interesting to note that dramatists and poets of later periods were supposed to be well versed in the *Kama-Sutra*, and frequently draw upon its contents in the delineation and treatment of their characters.

The Epics.—The beginnings of epic poetry in India go back to the period of the Vedas. At this time (*circa* 1000 B.C.) the art of narrative verse seems to have been familiar to the bards who attached themselves to the various small courts scattered up and down India, in which ballad singing and the recitation of old sagas and deeds of daring were regular occupations. The two great epics of India, the *Ramayana* (the adventures of Rama) and the *Mahabharata* (the great war of the Bharata family) are, therefore, merely a development of a tradition that was already well established in Indian literature. These epics throw a considerable amount of light upon the history and customs of the times. They contain chronological particulars of kings and their descendants and describe the conditions under which more ordinary people lived. The dates of the composition of these epics are a matter of controversy, but they may be safely referred to a period several centuries before the Christian era. Like the Homeric poems, however, which in several respects they resemble, they contain writings which appear to have been composed in different eras, new matter having been interpolated from time to time by the bards who recited them, a fact which makes it exceedingly difficult to attribute their authorship to any one person or period. Traditionally, however, Maharshi Vyasa is regarded as the author of the *Mahabharata* (although the name itself means 'a compiler'), and Valmiki as the author of the *Ramayana*. One of the outstanding characteristics of the epics is their enormous length. The *Mahabharata* consists of 220,000 sixteen-syllabled lines, and the *Ramayana* of 96,000 lines. They are often compared with the *Iliad* and the *Odyssey*, but the length of the *Mahabharata* alone, is nearly seven times that of the two Greek epics. Although both the epics belong to the class of literature known in India as Smitri or tradition rather than to that of Sruti or revelation, they are both regarded as sacred by millions of Hindus.

The story of the *Mahabharata* centres round the two rival dynasties, the Kauravas and the Pandavas, whose jealousy led to the great war of Kurukshetra, the legend of which still evokes admiration and veneration in the minds of Hindus. Although it is overweighted with lists of names and lineages, the *Mahabharata* is instinct throughout with pathos and tenderness and contains passages of great beauty.

The story of *Ramayana* is more compact; there is a more definite plot and the list of names and dates are fewer. This epic is divided into seven Kandas or Cantos, and relates the story of Rama, the crown prince of Ajoydhya, who is banished from his country, on account of the jealousy of his stepmother. He is followed into exile by his devoted wife Sita, who is regarded as embodying the ideal of Indian womanhood. Rama's younger brother, Lakshana, also follows him to the forest, and when the demon-king Ravana of Lanka (modern Ceylon) steals Sita, Lakshana helps his brother to raise an army to recover her; as a result Ravana is killed and Sita restored to her husband. From the purely literary point of view, the Ramayana may be regarded as transitional in form between the epic proper and the Kavyas of which we shall speak later.[1] The story itself is of unique interest, and its popularity amongst Indian readers is not inaptly anticipated by the following lines, with which the story begins:

> " As long as mountain ranges stand
> And rivers flow upon the earth
> So long will the *Ramayana*
> Survive upon the lips of men."

Buddhist Philosophical Literature.—Between the age of the epics and the golden age of Indian literature under the Guptas, there was a considerable output of literature whose purpose was to expound the philosophy of Buddhism. This literature, which was written not only in Sanskrit, but also in Pali (a popular form of Sanskrit), is to-day chiefly celebrated for the Jataka stories. A Jataka is a technical Buddhist name for a story in verse supposed to have been uttered by Buddha in one of his former incarnations. (These bodily manifestations in which Buddha is supposed to have been from time to time incarnated before his appearance in the sixth century as Buddha are known as Bodhisattvas.) The religious

[1] See below pp. 97, 98.

significance of the Jatakas derives from Buddha's traditional fondness for inserting them in his teaching, using them, as Christ used parables, to point a moral or to adorn a tale. The Jatakas, which cover a period of hundreds of years, are very various. There are fairy tales, anecdotes, comic lectures, and tales of adventure or romance. Many of them are animal stories. The Jatakas are written in a homely style and their quality of simple and direct narration gives them a certain literary value.

Other well-known works belonging to the literature of Buddhism are the *Dhammapada*, the Path of the Law, written about 70 B.C., and the *Ti-pitaka*, the Three Baskets, which is the name given to a collection of speeches, sayings, stories and reflections about Buddhism.

The Buddhist literature written in Pali, though extensive, is the product of a single school of Buddhists, the Hinayana school. Another school, the Mahayana, the Great Vehicle school, also produced a considerable Buddhist literature in Sanskrit. The most celebrated work of the Mahayana school is the *Buddha-Charita*, or life of Buddha in poetry, written by the greatest of the Mahayana teachers, Aswaghosha. Another famous Mahayana teacher, Nagarjuna, wrote the *Madyamaka-Karikas*, a systematic philosophical work also in verse. Both Nagarjuna and Aswaghosha were monks. Remarkable for erudition and breadth of vision, they laid down the main outlines of Buddhist philosophy and are held in great reverence by Buddhists all over the world.

The Gupta Period.—With the Gupta dynasty (*circa* A.D. 320) there began the great age of drama and lyric poetry in India known as "the Golden Age of the Guptas". The Golden Age was comparatively short. By A.D. 470 the Huns were already knocking at the gate of the North-west frontier and their incursions ultimately brought the greatest age of Indian civilisation to its close.

It so happens that there has come down to us from the seventh century a historical romance by a court poet called Bana. This work, intended for a biography of King Harsha (A.D. 606-648) vividly describes the life of the court and the army in Harsha's time, and contains a detailed account of the relations between the several sects of Buddhists and Hindus. Bana also wrote a romance entitled *Kadambari*, which he left incomplete. (It was afterwards finished by his son.) It is clear from Bana's work that under Harsha a certain degree of harmony and security had been re-established in Northern India. It is, however, also clear that the great age of Indian literature is already over; for Bana's writings are a typical product of a great period in decline. There is, for example, a loss of vitality for which the author seeks to compensate by an over-elaborate style. Rarely content with a single epithet, he introduces three or four where one would suffice. Bana palpably belongs to one of those silver ages of literature in which erudition takes the place of inspiration, and literature, like an over-ripe fruit, seems about to drop from a tree whose vitality is too weak to nourish it. By the seventh century A.D., then, the golden age of Indian literature was already past. What were the excellences in virtue of which this age, the age of the Guptas, obtained and deserved its epithet ?

Drama.—They were achieved primarily in the fields of drama and poetry, the two branches of literature which in the Gupta period came to their climax. It will be convenient to say something about each of them in turn. The origin of Indian drama, as of every other branch of Indian literature, can be traced to the Vedas. The earliest classical dramas, which have survived only in part, were written by the Buddhist monk, Aswaghosha, sometime during the first or second century A.D. By the fourth century A.D. the Indian drama had already acquired certain characteristic features which the Gupta dramatists further developed. For example, before a play begins a speaker is introduced who gives a short advance account of the drama that is to be unfolded and blesses the audience. This is called the benediction. Next there is a prologue, which consists usually of a dialogue between the manager and the chief actress on the theme of the play. Another characteristic feature is the insertion in the body of the play, which is usually written in Sanskrit, of dialect passages known as Prakrits. The art of acting was carefully studied during the Gupta period, and a number of books appeared on histrionic technique. In this connection it is worth noting that Indian producers anticipated the West by some thirteen hundred years in permitting women to play female parts. The first of the great dramatists of the Gupta period was Bhasa, who seems to have been writing about A.D. 350. Of his thirteen dramas, the *Daridra-charudatta*, and the *Svapna-vasavadatta* in six acts, are considered to be the greatest. Another important drama, of which the authorship is attributed to Bhasa, is the *Mricehakatika*, a story abounding with humour and variety of incident. Bhasa, however, is chiefly important because of his acknowledged influence upon Kalidasa, the greatest of the Indian dramatists.

Kalidasa.—Very little is known of the life of Kalidasa. It is most probable that he flourished under Chandragupta II of Ujjayini who ruled until about A.D. 413. His first dramatic work was the *Malavikagni-mitram*, a play in five acts. The theme of the play is a simple love story, but there is a number of purely humorous scenes and the whole play is pervaded by an atmosphere of happiness. The *Vikramorvashi*, the next play, shows a decided advance in imagination, but the perfection of Kalidasa's art is reached in the *Sakuntala*.

The story of the *Sakuntala* is delightfully simple. The king, Dushyanta, while on a hunting expedition, falls in love with Sakuntala, the daughter of a hermit. He marries her and goes away. A child is born and in due course the hermit, accompanied by the child's mother, takes it to court. The king, for reasons of policy, refuses to recognise the mother, but presently a divine voice bids him to acknowledge the child, and everything ends happily. The poet in this play excels himself in depicting the emotion of love: in particular, the scene in the fourth act in which the heroine, a woman sorrowful and tender, receives the loving farewell of the trees in the forest before she begins her journey to court, is acknowledged to be one of the finest in dramatic literature. The plot is technically well constructed, and a good deal of humour is introduced into the treatment of accidental scenes and minor characters. The style is highly finished. Vivid and beautiful, it achieves elegance without loss of strength and eloquence without sacrifice of precision. Kalidasa's work was not confined to drama.

He wrote some of the finest poetry in the world. The *Ritusamhara* (Cycle of the Seasons), the *Meghduta* (The Cloud Messenger), the *Kumarasambhava*, (Birth of the Prince) and the *Raghuvansha* (The Clan of the Raghus), four of his chief poetical works, are rich in imagination, glowing with warmth of feeling and instinct with the joy of life. The recognition of their importance is now world wide, but it is to Indians in particular that they appeal. To them they have, indeed, been a constant source of joy in every age.

Of the other dramatists of the Gupta period Bharavi, Bhatti, Kumaradasa, and Magha are the best known. They are sometimes known as the Kavya group and their writings as the Kavyas. Bharavi, who lived in the sixth century A.D., composed a dramatic poem in eighteen cantos, called the *Kiratarjuniya*, descriptive of the penance of Arjuna (a character from the *Mahabharata*). Bhatti, who lived about the middle of the seventh century, wrote among other works *Ravana Vadha*, or the Death of Ravana, and Kumaradasa, a contemporary admirer and imitator of Kalidasa, wrote *Janaki Harana*, a story in twenty cantos, dealing with the rape of Sita. Magha, who flourished in the latter part of the seventh century, is chiefly known for a work called the *Sisupalavadha* (The Death of Sisupala), a story borrowed from the *Mahabharata*.

Lyric Poets.—In addition to her dramatists, India has from time immemorial produced a great quantity of lyric poets. After the Vedas, upon whose lyrical qualities we have already commented, the first lyrical work that calls for notice is the poetry of Bhartrihari, who, writing in the seventh century A.D., produced work of exceptional grace and beauty. Bhartrihari wrote three *Satakas*, or Centuries of Verse, namely, the *Sringara-Sataka*, or Century of Love, the *Niti-Sataka*, or Century of Polity, and the *Vairagya-Sataka*, or Century of a Stilled Heart. In richness of imagination and wealth of description, these works are unsurpassed in Indian literature.

The next great writer of lyric verse, a Bengali named Jayadeva, flourished in the middle of the twelfth century, and was commonly spoken of as one of the five jewels of the court of Lakshanasena, the contemporary king of Bengal. His lyric opera, the *Gita Govinda*, or the Song of the Divine Cowherd, contains poems and songs of great beauty. It also provides for a number of dances. The story centres round the love affairs of Radha and Krishna, the two popular deities of Hindu mythology. The story of beautiful Radha—

> "Jasmine-bosomed Radha
> All in the springtime waited by the wood
> For Krishna fair, Krishna the all-forgetful
> Krishna with earthly love's false fire consuming"

—has continued to please the people of India in every age, while its ecstatic lyrical quality has won the admiration of scholars and lovers of literature all over the world.

Fables.—A survey of ancient Indian literature would be incomplete without some mention of the beast fables and children's stories which are very common in the early writings. One of the most famous fables is the *Panchatantra* or "Book of the Five Heads", which dates from a very early period. The five subjects dealt with in the book are as follows: (1) The loss of Friends, (2) The winning of Friends, (3) Crows and Owls, (4) The loss of gains, and (5) Ill-considered action. The writer's purpose is to relate anecdotes of animal behaviour, from which may be drawn morals applicable to the everyday life of human beings. Consequently the fables are written in a simple conversational style. The *Hitopadesha*, or the Book of Good Counsel, is considerably later than the *Panchatantra*, and many of the fables which it contains have been incorporated into the literature of Europe. Some bear a striking resemblance to the fables of Aesop. They are of a charming simplicity, and are especially enjoyed by the children, for whom they were intended.

Romances.—Differing very little from the fables, except that they are intended for grown-ups, are the tales and romances which began to be popular in India as a form of entertainment in the eleventh century. Of these Kshemendra's *Brihat Kathamanjari*, or The Great Cluster of Stories in eighteen books, written between A.D. 1020 and 1040, is one of the best-known. Primarily a book of adventures, it is distinguished by an elaborate psychological study, one of the first in literature, of the hero. Perhaps the most famous of the romances is Somadeva's *Kathasaritsagar*, or Oceans of the Rivers of Story, written between A.D. 1063 and 1081. This is a huge work of 21,500 slokas or couplets, containing an enormous number of tales and fantasies somewhat after the manner of the *Arabian Nights Entertainment*.

Mediæval and Modern Period.—During the period of the Mohammedan invasions, the continuity of Indian literature seems to have been broken. So soon, however, as the Mohammedans had begun to settle down in India, and an environment of comparative tranquillity had been established, a movement began for the revival and reformulation of the traditional Hindu religion, which found a considerable literary expression, chiefly in poetry. The language chosen as the vehicle for this expression was no longer Sanskrit, but the vernaculars of the provinces to which the various authors who composed the movement belonged. In Bengal this movement of revival took on the character of a protest against the decadence of Hindu society. Its leader, Chaitanya, known as the founder of the Vaishnava movement (A.D. 1485–1534), was a poet of very considerable accomplishment, the first of a long line of Vaishnava poets who over a period of centuries devoted themselves to the cult of the ancient Hindu religion and, writing in mediæval Bengali, produced a poetry which derived its inspiration from religious ecstasy. Even the work of the minor members of this school contains passages of the greatest beauty. The Bengali movement was in no sense an isolated one. From 1450 onwards Northern India was swept by a series of religious revivals, each of which received interpretation from an attendant body of poets. Of these poets of the cult of devotional religion the greatest was Tulsi Das (1532 to 1624), whose translation of the *Ramayana* into Hindustani made the epic accessible to the masses of people who were unable to read Sanskrit. In the south the most famous of the religious poets was Tuka-Ram, who belonged to the Vaishnava school. These were poets of the religion of Hinduism proper, but Kabir (1440 to 1518), a poet of Northern India, whose passionate and mystical devotion gave to Indian literature a new direction, wrote with the avowed purpose of effecting a reconciliation between the Hindu and the Mohammedan religions. Kabir's efforts in this direction were not without success; indeed, he played a considerable part in bridging the gulf which has separated the two major religions of India.

Mohammedan Literature.—The Mohammedan literature of the Middle Ages consists mostly of history and biography. The Emperor Babur's *Memoirs* contain the personal impressions and acute reflections of a cultivated man of the world. Two brothers, Faizi, the poet, and Abul Fazl, the historian, who were at Akbar's court and wrote in Persian, have also left valuable records of the time. Abul Fazl composed works entitled *Akbar Nama*, the Life of Akbar, and *Ain-i-Akbari*, the Institutes of Akbar. These works contain an account of Akbar's reign, and describe the legislation which he passed with the avowed intention of benefiting the people. Another important work of a later period, also written in Persian, is the *Dabistan*, by a Mohammedan judge called Muhsin-i-Fani, who was in office under the Emperor Shah Jehan in the late seventeenth century.

The Sixteenth Century and After.—From the sixteenth century onwards, Indian literature, which had hitherto been written almost entirely in Sanskrit, increasingly finds its natural expression in the dialects of the various peoples of India, and works appear in Hindustani, in Marathi and in Bengali.

With the advent of the European peoples, the literature of India received a new stimulus which found expression in a series of diaries describing day-to-day Indian life. Apart from the diarists both European and Indian, there have been numerous Indian and Anglo-Indian writers who have felt drawn towards India and have sought to express their feeling for Indian life and culture in English. Prominent among these Anglo-Indian writers was Sir Edwin Arnold, whose celebrated poem, *The Light of Asia*, was inspired by India. Better known still is the work of Henri Derozio, whose *Fakir of Jungheera* palpably derives from Indian sources, and is influenced by Indian models. Rabindranath Tagore is a contemporary Bengali poet whose work has achieved world-wide celebrity. He is a writer of prolific genius and his dramas, novels and philosophical discourses are almost as well known as his poetry. Sarojini Naidu, the Indian poetess, has also produced first-rate work. She belongs to a school of young modern writers whose work is characterised by an energy and vigour that suggest a definite renaissance of Indian literature. Like so much of the work of the twentieth century, the plays and novels of this school are realistic, even at times satirical, in character, and inevitably they are preoccupied with political and social issues. But the fact that much of this work is propagandist in intention does not detract from the excellence of the result.

CHAPTER V

THE ART OF GOVERNMENT

To the art of politics, the art which seeks to prescribe how men shall best live together in communities, it cannot be said that India has made any outstanding contribution. Indian thought has in general been more concerned with the good life for the individual, than with the good life for the community; and the good life for the individual, Indian philosophy has taught, is not to be realised in communities of citizens but in the apotheosis of souls. It is, perhaps, partly for this reason that Indians have usually been badly governed and have been and are exceedingly poor. Since, however, no story of Indian civilisation would be complete without some account of Indian political history, the following brief sketch may be of interest to those who wish to know how India has been governed in the past, and what are the problems that confront her citizens in the present and the immediate future.

The Societies of Mohenjo Daro.—The earliest forms of society of which we have any record are those which flourished in the cities of Mohenjo Daro and Harappa in the Punjab, to which reference has already been made,[1] about 4000 or 3000 B.C.—that is to say, long before the Aryan invaders

[1] See Chapter I, p. 1, and Chapter III, pp. 65, 66.

settled in India. Recent excavations have disclosed a certain amount of information as to the mode of life of their inhabitants. Archæologists have in particular been impressed by the absence of remains of weapons of offence and defence. The ruins of these well-planned cities show no traces of the walls, ramparts, or fortifications, which appear almost invariably among the ruins of the other early settlements of our race. The inference is drawn that these early societies, the earliest in India of which we have any record, were comparatively free from the fear of violence and war.

How, the question inevitably presents itself, did these Indian communities succeed in dispensing with those means of defence of which almost all the early societies of mankind seem to have felt the need ? Presumably, by virtue of being ignorant of war. They neither feared nor performed violence. But how comes it, then, that war, the scourge of mankind, left this early Indian civilisation untouched ? All known human societies seem to have been based on force within and to have feared force from without, and, what is more, the earlier the society, the more universal, the more persistent the evidences of fighting.

A Special Psychological Technique.—A recent writer [1] has made an interesting suggestion to account for this peculiarity of early Indian societies. Its explanation, he holds, is to be found in the practice of a certain psychological technique which was discovered in India at a very early date and

[1] Gerald Heard in his book, *The Source of Civilisation.*

which has never been entirely lost. By virtue of this technique, the peoples of these early civilisations, not only in India proper but also in Egypt and Mesopotamia, had developed their consciousness in such a way that violence of any kind was abhorrent to it. What this technique may have been is pure conjecture, conjecture which belongs to the province of psychology rather than to that of history. One suggestion is, however, that whereas the personality of most people is to-day split into two parts, the conscious and the unconscious, which are separated by a definite gulf, the personalities of the men of these early civilisations were integrated wholes in which no such fissure occurred. Yet, while removing the will to violence, the integration of personality so happily achieved does not seem to have withdrawn, men's attention from the duties of our common life in the everyday world. Such a withdrawal whose advocacy was a feature of subsequent Indian philosophies also makes for pacifism, but it is, many would hold, a pacifism purchased at too high a price.

The suggestion just made is supported by the circumstance that the ruins of these early cities lack temples, palaces and municipal buildings as well as walls and fortifications. Their inhabitants, that is to say, apparently dispensed with gods and the machinery of religion, no less than with rulers and the machinery of government. What *has* been found is an engraved seal which is supposed to represent Siva, the Prince of the Yogis. The presence of this seal certainly suggests that mystical practices were known to the people of this early civilisation, and strengthens the conjecture that it was by mystical methods that they succeeded in avoiding the constant violence to which other early communities of mankind have been so lamentably and so universally addicted. The existence of this psychological technique may also go some way to explain the absence of religious persecution in India, the willingness to live and let live, and the readiness to adopt an attitude of stoical resignation to adversity, to which in the preceding pages I have drawn attention.

The Vedic Assemblies.—In previous chapters I have on a number of occasions referred to the Vedas and the Upanishads. Apart from their literary and philosophical importance, these writings possess interest as constituting the earliest *written* record of Indian life. The communities they describe are popular and democratic, the will of the people finding expression in elected assemblies and democratically governed institutions. The most important institution of this kind was called the Samiti, which was later known as the Panchayat.

The Samiti and its Functions.—The word Samiti means " meeting together ", and the Samiti was, therefore, an assemblage or assembly. Every group of villages had its Samiti, whose members consisted of delegates or representatives from the different villages in the group, the village representatives being known as Gramani. Historians have deduced from a number of scattered references that the Samiti elected a king for the group of villages which it represented. It could also, apparently, recall a king who had been banished. From references in the *Rig-Veda* it appears that the king's duties included attendance at the Samiti. A good king did, in fact, always attend, and a constitutional precedent was thus established. The Samiti conceded the right of free expression and open discussion to all its members, and its usual procedure was by way of debate. Considered as an assembly for the conduct of public business it was, indeed, at a substantially higher level of development than the folk assemblies of the early Middle Ages in Europe. Nor were its discussions purely political; social and religious matters also fell within its province. The Samiti began to disappear after the rise of the Empires in 650 B.C. and from 500 B.C. onwards, references to them in Indian literature are always in the past tense.

The Sabha, Vidatha and Sena.—Another feature of the social organisation of the Vedic age was the Sabha, a word which means literally "a body of men shining together", and conveys the suggestion that those who were entitled to a seat in the Sabha were thereby invested with lustre. The Sabha seems to have been a sort of standing committee of selected persons of the kind whom the English call "elder statesmen", appointed by the Samiti and acting under its supervision as the judicature of the community. The religious life of the community was organised through the assembly known as the Vidatha, which also performed certain civil and military functions. The Sena, or army, which was in these early times more or less identical with the whole community in arms, ranked as a separate constitutional unit.

Buddhist Period. 500 B.C. to A.D. 200.—The

main sources of our information for the Buddhist period, which lasted roughly for seven hundred years—from 500 B.C. to A.D. 200—are a number of books of commentary upon the Vedic literature known as the *Dharma-Sutras*, composed by Gautama (not to be confused with Gautama Buddha). Information is also contained in the *Jatakas* or Legends. Though the Legends deal with the Buddhist period, they contain a number of references to the state of India during the centuries preceding Buddha. From the scattered references in the *Jatakas* and from the accounts contained in the *Dharma-Sutras*, we gather that up to the time of Buddha the Samiti and the Sabha continued to function with very little change. We now hear, however, for the first time of provision for the education of the community. This appears to have been organised in bodies called Charanas, which broadly corresponded to the modern conception of faculties. The main function of the Charanas was to teach the doctrines of the Vedas. We hear also of trade guilds, consisting of the merchants belonging to a particular trade or profession, and of merchant guilds consisting of those belonging to all the trades or professions in a particular locality. The mention of these guilds suggest that village life was already beginning to give way to town life.

The Hindu Republics: 500 B.C. to A.D. 350.—The early Vedas only mention elected monarchs. The characteristic form of government of post-Vedic times is Republicanism. Megasthenes,[1] writing

[1] See Chapter I, p. 7.

about 300 B.C., records that sovereignty (kingship) was dissolved and that democratic governments were set up in a number of places.

The historians of Alexander's campaign also mention a number of States as " free, autonomous and independent ". Thus when Alexander reached the Beas, he heard that beyond that river the country was populated by a people who were ruled by an aristocratical form of government.

During his retreat Alexander actually came across a number of Indian republics. Indeed, all the States with which he made contact on his way back along the Indus appear to have been under republican forms of government. The most powerful of these were the Khudrakas and the Malavas. From the descriptions in the writings of Greek historians, we gather that the populations of the republics were large, their territories wide; that they contained numbers of cities and that some of them were very rich. In a word they were independent, wealthy, prosperous and highly organised.

The Buddha himself was born in a republican country, and it is not without significance that he should have called the monastic order he founded the Republic of the Bhikkus (Monks), the name " Republic " suggesting that he transferred the constitution of a political to a religious order.

There is, indeed, ample evidence to show that the early Buddhist orders lived under a republican form of government, to which circumstance many ascribe their continued existence during so many centuries.

The Decline of the Republics.—To return to politics, independent democratic and aristocratic republics seem to have flourished widely throughout the continent of India for a period of nearly a thousand years, a period which ended with the establishment of the Gupta Empire in A.D. 320. They existed, that is to say, side by side with the Maurya Empire and its successors, which seem in general to have refrained from any interference with the republics. What were the main characteristics of these petty states?

The outstanding feature of the republican system during the Buddhist period is that known as the "gana rajya", or rule of numbers, that is to say, the rule of many persons. In spite of this alleged "gana rajya", however, the republics seem to have been more or less aristocratic or oligarchic in character, and to have resembled in their general features the city states of ancient Greece and Rome and the mercantile towns of mediæval Italy and the Hanseatic League. Kautilya, the contemporary historian of the Maurya Empire (500 to 400 B.C.), affirms in his *Artha-Shastra*[1] that the imperial policy towards the republics was one of toleration. Nevertheless, throughout the period of the Maurya Empire and its successors the importance of the republics gradually diminished, and they were finally absorbed into the Gupta Empire about A.D. 350. The fact is not surprising. It must have required constant vigilance on the part of a small republic to defend its freedom against a large empire, and, if the *Artha-Shastra* is believed, the republics found it

[1] See Chapter IV, pp. 88, 89.

necessary to conscript all their citizens in their defence. The fact that each petty republican state was increasingly a nation in arms, led to internal disorder, besides provoking, as it has always done in history, the external wars against which the arms were intended to serve as a protection. While the Maurya emperors seem to have acquiesced in the continuance of those republics which were individually strong, or which had acquired strength through being united in leagues with other republics, those which were weakened by a policy of internal division were gradually annexed. The enlightened policy followed by Asoka's government (274 B.C. to 237 B.C.) induced most of the republics which had survived to submit without a struggle. The result was the establishment of a strong central government, which extended as far as Persia in the north-west and the Tamil country in the south, under which India achieved such unity and peace as she had never before known. The nature of Asoka's Empire was that of a loose federation rather than of an Empire in the commonly accepted sense of the word. The republics seem to have formed part of this Empire, while retaining their individualities and a considerable part of their independence.

Under the rule of the Gupta Empire the republics, with two exceptions, finally disappeared. The exceptions were the Lichchavis republic and the republic founded by Pushya Mitra in Rajputana about A.D. 450. Pushya Mitra was strong enough to administer a severe defeat to the imperial forces under Kumara Gupta, a defeat which nearly destroyed the Gupta dynasty. The army of the Lichchavis republic was beaten by the imperial forces towards the end of the fifth century, although the republic itself does not seem to have become entirely absorbed in the Empire for a considerable period.

Republics and Empires contrasted.—By the end of the fifth century A.D. the republics had finally disappeared from India, and the republican form of government, which had subsisted unchanged from the time of the Vedas, had given place to a different conception of the State, the conception which is embodied in the word, Empire. The virtue of the Empire lies in its unifying effect. It brings many people under the control of a single authority and establishes over a wide area common laws, customs and institutions, sustained by a strong central government. But its virtues entail corresponding defects. The larger the unit of administration, the more remote is it from the people whose affairs it administers. The more centralised the government, the less directly does it represent those whom it is its business to govern. Democratic and republican governments may be weak and strife-torn; but they do tend to maintain contact with those whose existence is at once the cause and the justification of there being government at all, namely, the people who are being governed. The pages of subsequent Indian history are studded with great names—great statesmen, great emperors, great writers and great thinkers. But after the fall of the republics in the fifth century A.D. we do not seem again to hear of the Indian people. And for a good reason; for at no subsequent period have the people been admitted to a share in the government, nor have they at any subsequent time played a prominent part in the life of the country. From the Gupta period onwards the system of government in India becomes increasingly complex and, therefore, increasingly bureaucratic at the centre, while at the circumference, the village communities, which had once been independent republics and in which the real life of the country still went on, were left increasingly to look after themselves. Remote from the sources of power, they were made aware of the existence of government only when they were called upon to pay taxes and to provide levies.

The Peace of the " World Ruler ".—It is after the downfall of the republics and their gradual absorption into the Gupta Empire, that we first meet with the idea of the Sarva-Bhauma or " World Ruler " in Indian political thought. This is a conception for which India must share the credit, if, indeed, credit is rightly due—for why, it may be asked, should anybody aspire to rule the world ?—with Rome. The Indians, like the Romans, identified the geographical area with which they happened to be immediately acquainted, with the world, and, as in Rome, the idea of the " World Ruler " arose from the unification of a very considerable territory under a single government which remained stable for a comparatively lengthy period. The ruler of this territory was said to " rule the world ". If he was moderately successful in suppressing strife within his dominions, he was further said to have given the world peace. In India such conditions lasted for a period of some three hundred years, during which there was a succession of " World Rulers ".

The Southern Andhra Empire (240 B.C. — A.D. 250) *and the Kusana Empire*.—Meanwhile in the south there had grown up during the five hundred years, 240 B.C. to A.D. 250, the Empire of the Andhras, who maintained commercial intercourse with Western Asia, Greece, Rome, Egypt and China. In the north, their rivals in pre-Gupta times were the Indo-Tartars, or Kusanas, who had commercial and diplomatic relations with the Han Empire of China and with the Roman Empire. Their most famous monarch, Kaniska (A.D. 78 to 123), was a contemporary of Trajan and Hadrian.

The Gupta Empire and Peace.—To the Kusans there succeeded in Northern India the Guptas, whose capital was at Pataliputra (modern Patna) and under whose rule Hindu culture began to spread far beyond the boundaries of India. In particular, Hindu influence served to bring about the Chinese renaissance of the Tang period (A.D 618 to 905) and thus indirectly assisted in the emergence of Japan as a separate civilised state. The Gupta Empire was a highly efficient administrative machine extending its sphere of operations over an ever-growing area of Indian life. Each of the Gupta emperors regarded himself as a " world ruler " and conferred upon himself a title which was intended to symbolise the peace and security by which he conceived his rule to be distinguished. The Gupta emperors did not, however, find it necessary to have recourse to the Roman expedient of setting up a number of puppet kings to maintain their authority in regions which were not technically parts of the Empire, and succeeded for the most part in keeping peace and order throughout the country as a whole by a system of provincial governors.

A frequent though by no means an invariable consequence of a peaceful and ordered society is an outburst of self-expression in literature and the other creative arts. Freed from fear, indifferent to military glory, economically secure, men and women have at once the leisure and the desire to seek expression in literature and to create beautiful things. So it was in India under the Guptas. The age of the Guptas has already been referred to as the Golden Age of Indian culture.[1] It was the great age of Indian art and thought, an age which, it is interesting to note, was contemporary with the beginning of the Dark Ages in Europe, when civilisation to all intents and purposes disappeared, and Europe was submerged in the darkness of a chaos lit only by the sombre fires of brutality.

The size of these Indian Empires offers an interesting comparison with that of other great Empires of the past. It is computed that the area of the Maurya Empire in, say, 400 B.C., was considerably greater than that of the Roman Empire at its height during the second and third centuries A.D., and that the Gupta Empire, even during the period of its decline, was larger than the Franco-German Empire of Charlemagne.

[1] See Chapter IV, pp. 94, 95.

Vardhanas and Chalukyas.—The Gupta Empire was finally disrupted by the challenge of the Empire of the *Vardhanas* (A.D. 606-647), in Northern India, with its capital at Kanauj, and of the Empire of the Chalukyas with its capital at Vatapi, the city now known as Badami in Bijupur, in the south.

Disintegration of the Empires.—By the seventh and eighth centuries the great Empires had begun to break up, and out of their ruins was formed a multitude of small States. The area which the sentiment of national patriotism now considered to be within its scope considerably contracted. Men no longer thought in terms of a single hegemony extending over the whole of India, and the small independent monarchies which now sprang up all over the country monopolised their loyalties. The five chief national groupings of this period were, first, the Pala and Sena Emperors of Bengal (730-1200); secondly, the Gurjara-Prathiharas of Upper India and Rajputana (816-1194). A third Empire was that of the Rashtrakutas of the Deccan (750-973). These had overthrown the Chalukyas, and their ruler, Govinda III, had given himself the title of Sarva Bhauma of the south. The supremacy of the Rashtrakutas was successfully challenged by the Empire of the Cholas (850-1310). A fifth Empire, the kingdom of Kashmir, emerged about 650 in the north and lasted for about seven hundred years.

The Mohammedan Period.—The Gurjara-Prathiharas submitted to the Mohammedans in 1194, the Senas in 1200, the kingdom of Kashmir in 1339 and the Cholas in 1310. The submission of the Cholas marks the end of the period of the Hindu Empires, but their sovereignty did not disappear without a struggle. There was resistance on the part of the Bengali king, Danuja-Mardana (A.D. 1417) who fought for control of Bengal and of the Rajput States in the middle-west. The Empire of Vijayanagar resisted the Mohammedans for over two hundred years, 1336 to 1565, while in the Deccan Sivaji maintained his independence until well on into the seventeenth century, and the Mahrattas in the north-west until the eighteenth. Part of the Mahratta Empire, indeed, still remains scattered over Central and North-western India in the form of ostensibly Native States, which are in fact largely dependent upon Great Britain. The case of the Mahrattas was, however, exceptional, and by the seventeenth century Moslem supremacy had been firmly established in India, and the Indo-Saracenic renaissance in art and letters was well under way. During the whole of this period of some five hundred years, during which Hindu and Moslem struggled for supremacy, no part of India came under the rule of a foreign power. The Mogul emperors were not foreigners governing a subject people. On the contrary, they were as completely Indian as the great Hindu emperors whom they superseded, and although there were instances of bigotry and intolerance on the part of some of these Mohammedan rulers, the policy of the Moslem Empire was on the whole liberal and tolerant. As a general rule it interfered neither with the local administration nor with the religious customs of the people under its control.

The Village Communes.—In spite of the rise and fall of empires and dynasties, India has kept her tradition of village autonomy almost intact. Village autonomy constitutes, indeed, the one continuing and stable feature of the social life of India. Before the era of the empires, these communes were, as we have seen, independent in every sense of the word. The village assemblies, assisted by the Sabhas, the Vidathas and the Senas, performed between them all the functions of government, deliberative, judicial, military and political. These early communes were fully developed democracies, the State being synonymous with the village or group of villages. The government was the village assembly, the king of the village or group and his ministers forming a quasi permanent executive. At this stage, then, the distinction between central and local government does not arise. All governments were local, and managed the entire life of the community under their control. Santhagaras, or public halls, rest-houses and reservoirs were constructed by the co-operative effort of the villagers themselves. Nor was this co-operation in communal works confined to men; women also took part in works of public utility and village enterprise.

With the coming of the empires, the functions of government became increasingly centralised, and many of the powers and duties of administration passed out of the control of the village communes. Nevertheless, the tradition of village self-rule persisted, and although, so far at any rate as Northern India was concerned, their importance was much diminished, the village communes continued to function throughout the period of the Guptas and the Moguls. In Southern India they appear to have retained a considerably larger proportion of their functions. Thus we have records of no less than forty villages in which, during the reign of the Chola emperor, Raja-Raja I (A.D. 985 to 1018), the inhabitants managed their own affairs, the Panchayat, or general assembly, administering the business of the village as a whole, and dividing itself into a number of sub-committees or sub-Panchayats for special purposes.

Constitution of Panchayat.—The method of election to the Panchayat was partly democratic and partly dependent upon chance. There were two qualifications for membership. An intending member must be under seventy-five and over thirty years of age, and he must possess a certain amount of property which was exactly specified. It must, for example, include more than one and a quarter acres of tax-paying land and a dwelling house built on the owner's estate.

The following account describes the system of election in a particular village. "The village with its twelve streets was divided into thirty wards. Everyone who lived in these wards wrote a name on a ticket. The tickets were first arranged in separate bundles representing the thirty wards. Each bundle bore the name to which it belonged. The bundles were then collected and put into a pot and placed before the general body of inhabitants both young and old in meeting assembled. All the priests were required to be present. The oldest priest then took the pot, and looking upwards so as to be seen by all the people, called upon one of the young boys standing close by to pick out one of the bundles. The tickets in this bundle were then removed to another pot. After it had been well shuffled, the boy took one ticket out of this bundle and handed it to an officer, called the arbitrator, who received it in the palm of his hand with fingers open. He read out the name, which was then shouted out by the priests."[1] Women could become members of the Panchayats and inscriptions contain references to women members of the village Sabhas. Officers appointed from among members of the Panchayats for the performance of special duties held office for a period of one year only. Some were elected; in other cases the appointment was made by lot. After a year's tenure of office the holder vacated it and passed on to another, thus gaining varied experience of civic administration.

Functions of the Panchayat.—Besides administering the affairs of the village, the Panchayats were absolute proprietors of its land and possessed rights of ownership over all newly cleared lands. They imposed and collected taxes and could, if they chose, declare a village tax free. They were also authorised to take possession of and to sell the land of peasants who had failed to pay their taxes over a period of three years. They were responsible for the administration of local justice, and adjudicated upon all crimes from petty theft to murder.

[1] From an inscription found at Uttaramallur, quoted by Professor R. K. Mookerjee in his book *Local Government in Ancient India*.

As we have seen, the political status of the village declined from the beginning of the Gupta Empire. From being free and independent city or village states, they became provincial units of the central government. Nevertheless they did, in fact, remain units, retaining many of their judicial and administrative functions, and altering their procedure from time to time to adjust themselves to new political conditions. On these lines they have continued right up to the present day. The village communities thus embody a continuing tradition of local self-government, extending for a period of nearly three thousand years.

Present State of Village Communes.—The survival of the Panchayat system in face of the highly centralised power of imperial governments bears striking testimony to the policy of non-interference and toleration pursued by the rulers of India, and not only by the Hindu emperors, but also by the Moguls. Rural India has to a surprising extent remained unaffected by the political changes through which the country as a whole has passed. Villages still very largely govern themselves, and the tradition of self-government and co-operative effort which has been handed down from a past immeasurably remote, persists practically unchanged. The fact that these village communities are the repositories of such an ancient tradition has its bad as well as its good side. It is good that there should be continuity with the past, especially in the case of a community which is rooted in the soil. It is good, too, that the village should be self-governing. But it is bad that it should be without drains, and that, partly because it is without drains, the infant mortality rate should be in the neighbourhood of twenty-six per cent. To permit twenty-six out of every hundred babies born to die in their first year of life is literally to sacrifice human lives upon the altar of tradition; for it is the persistence of tradition that offers to any proposed alteration in the way of life of the villages a disabling opposition. "Our fathers did not have these things. Why, then, should we?" Such is the instinctive attitude of the tradition-bound Indian peasant. Resistant to material improvements, the villagers are no less distrustful of new ideas. Indian life, to-day, is thus like a mosaic whose pieces are little, solid, isolated blocks. As a result, the average Indian village is conservative, ridden by disease, and very poor, so poor, that, as we shall see in the next chapter, villagers in increasing numbers are being driven to migrate to the towns. It is only too probable that the conservatism is, at least in part, the cause of the poverty and the disease. If, indeed, we were to venture to make a criticism of the Indian contribution to the art of government as a whole, it would not be very different from that which has been suggested by our survey of Indian philosophical and religious thought. In its pre-occupation with the large and the remote, Indian thought is over much given to despising the humble and the trivial. Focussing its attention upon the pilgrimage of man's soul to another world, Indian religion has given too little attention to the life of his body in this one. Concerned to maintain its traditions and its independence, Indian local government has paid too little attention to its lavatories and drains. It is a pity. The issues raised by this stricture will be treated in greater detail in the next chapter, where I shall seek to show that the apparent opposition between material well-being and spiritual insight is in no sense necessary. Indeed, it should not be necessary to invoke the celebrated Indian principle of unity in difference, to affirm the obvious truth that it is the same fundamental reality which expresses itself at once in the activity of man's spirit and in the well-being of his body.

India and the Right to Self-Government.—Before I bring this chapter to a close, it seems appropriate, since its subject is India's contribution to the art of government, to say something on the vexed question of India's right to, and India's capacity for, self-government.

It is sometimes said that Indians, besides being *temperamentally* unfitted to exercise the functions of government, are in a peculiarly eminent degree incapacitated for the active conduct of affairs by the distinctive Hindu view of life which, regarding the emancipation of the soul from the ambitions and desires of this world as the goal of existence, affects an attitude of indifference—even of reprobation—to worldly activity and worldly success.

Apart from the fact that government is an art which is acquired by practice, and that no people can, therefore, be regarded as fit for self-government, unless it is first given the opportunity to fit itself by governing itself, the charge is based upon a misconception of the Hindu view of life. In Chapter II[1] I described the four stages of the life of man envisaged by the traditional Indian philosophy. Of these the third and fourth, Vanaprasthya and Sanyasa, prescribe, the third, retirement from public duties, and the fourth, preparation for the departure of the soul. But the retirement of stage three is partial and gradual only, whilst the first and second stages recommend a full-blooded worldly activity.

It is true that during the last four or five hundred years a fatalistic quietism has only too often been permitted to pervade the Indian's attitude to mundane affairs and worldly duties *throughout the whole of his life*; that stage four, in other words, has been treated as if it comprised the whole span of existence, so that India has languished within the shadow of a great renunciation. But this is a perversion of Hindu doctrine for which the main body of Indian philosophy affords no justification; nor is there any religious or metaphysical reason why, given the opportunity for a life of active and fruitful participation in the affairs of the community, Indians should reject it, or, having accepted it, acquit themselves therein less creditably than other peoples.

A Policy for the Empire.—It is, indeed, difficult to resist the conclusion that in the present world situation a policy of generous concession to Indian aspirations accords no less with the demands of expediency than with the claims of justice. The British have been disposed to put too little trust in the people of India. Treating them as unwilling

[1] See Chapter II, p. 29.

subjects in the present, they have been only too ready to regard them in the light of potential enemies in the future, fearing lest, should an emergency arise, they will hasten to seek the support of any Asiatic power who might assist them to throw off the British yoke. So long as the policy of Great Britain in relation to India remains one of coercion tempered by niggling concessions, such apprehensions may well be justified. A policy of trust introduced with a few generous gestures in regard to matters which Indians regard as important, such as, for example, the reduction of Civil Service salaries, the granting of an amnesty to political prisoners, or the expenditure of increased revenue upon the social services, would go far to remove the causes of this just apprehension. A similar policy pursued after the Boer War was more than justified by its results. Nor can it reasonably be doubted that, if Indians were asked to co-operate on equal terms in the administration and defence of their country, instead of being treated as ill-conditioned subordinates on the look-out for opportunities of recalcitrance, they would be willing to repay trust with service and rally to the defence of the Empire in the East in any emergency that might arise through the aggressive policy of unsatisfied Asiatic powers.

CHAPTER VI

THE IMPACT OF THE WEST

Introductory.—In this final chapter I propose to say something about the effect upon Indian civilisation of contact with the West, to make a brief survey of India's condition in the present, and to estimate her prospects in the immediate future. Of the effects of contact with the West, some are good, others bad. It will be convenient to consider both the good and the bad, first, in the realm of matter, and secondly, in that of the spirit. In the first connection, I shall seek to estimate the credit and debit side of the partial industrialisation of India, that is to say, of the railways, roads, factories, hospitals, and irrigation works, which have resulted from India's contact with the West. In the second, I shall treat of some of the effects upon the traditional Indian philosophy and the characteristic Hindu attitude to life of the widely different standards and valuations of nineteenth and twentieth century Europe.

Haphazard Origin of Connection with the West.—No one would deny the far-reaching character of the effects upon India of her contact with the West. Yet the establishment of Europeans in India was a curiously haphazard affair. The British, for example, did not originally come to India in pursuance of plans of Empire, nor had the East India

Company, when in 1641 it set up its first trading station in India, any thought of interference with the internal affairs of the country. The diffident spirit which inspired these early approaches of the West to India is well illustrated by the tone of the letter in which John Russell, the President of the East India Company, applied in 1713 for trading rights, to the Emperor Farakhsiwar, a letter in which he ingratiatingly describes himself as "the smallest particle of sand, John Russell, President of the East India Company (with his forehead at command rubbed on the ground)".[1] In 1715, after waiting two years at the Emperor's Court, an embassy sent under John Surman obtained the right of free trading in Bengal.

The story of the rise of British power in India from these humble foundations is familiar, and need not be re-told here. Powerful factors operating in favour of the invaders were afforded by the conditions prevailing in India at the time. The English came at a fortunate moment. The Indian political system which had lasted for so many centuries was gradually decaying. The Imperial government had lost its hold over the subsidiary provincial governments, and the governors of many of the provinces were openly defying its authority. Meanwhile one provincial power fought against another, and India was rent with civil war. In the North-west the Mahrattas were carrying out a series of raids, each of which left the Imperial government weaker than the last. More damaging

[1] Thompson and Garratt, *Rise and Fulfilment of British Rule in India*, p. 55.

even than the Mahrattas were the Persians. Nadir Shah had invaded India from Persia in 1738 and, having stormed Delhi, massacred its inhabitants. After this last invasion, the Mogul Empire, already tottering to its fall, to all intents and purposes ceased to exist. It was precisely at this juncture that the East India Company ceased to be a purely trading concern and decided to make a bid for political influence. The British did not, then, acquire their Empire in India as part of a deliberately pursued policy of conquest. Their intervention was an accident which fate turned into an Empire. In the political drama of the next two hundred years the English assume the leading rôle, but the Indians had already set the stage. To the examination of the consequences of this, one of the most momentous accidents of history, I now turn.

Unmixed Material Benefits.—Let us consider, first, those consequences which may be regarded as unmixed goods. These are largely such as may be classed as material. There has been progress in the conquest of disease. India, before the arrival of the English invasion, did not possess a system of sanitation, and medical science, as the West conceives it, was practically non-existent. There are no figures for Indian mortality before the coming of the English in the eighteenth century, but it is clear that they must have been very high.

The land has been irrigated. Great tracts of India have in the past suffered severely from drought. From the time of the first settlement of the East India Company the English have made more or less continuous efforts to diminish its worst effects by irrigation works. Prior to 1918 some £74,000,000 had been spent on this work, and it has been estimated that 21,000,000 acres of land had as a result been brought under cultivation. Since the war expenditure under this head has increased. The cost of irrigation projects sanctioned since 1919 is estimated at some £49,000,000, and they are expected to make available for cultivation another 13,000,000 acres. Railways have been constructed. Nearly 42,000 miles of railways have been built in India during the last hundred years, and they are now carrying over 600,000,000 passengers a year (at an average charge of about a third of a penny a mile) and nearly 90,000,000 tons of goods. Only two countries in the world have a larger railway mileage.

It may be objected that the motives which led the British to undertake these material improvements were not wholly, or even mainly, altruistic. Their purposes, it may be said, were, first, to develop the country in their own interests, and, secondly, to secure a good return on the capital which they had subscribed. This no doubt is true. It may be said, further, that the public works to which reference has been made would in any event have been undertaken. Asiatic nations which have remained independent, such as China, Japan and Persia, also have railways, and it is unlikely that India would have remained completely cut off from Western science and Western industry, or that Indian resources should have remained completely unexploited by Western capital. Already in the eighteenth century movements which threatened India's isolation were under way, and, even if the British had not come, contact with the West would have been established as a result of India's own initiative.

All this, no doubt, is true. Nevertheless, it may, I think, fairly be urged that the irrigation and transport systems are because of British rule more extensive and more efficient than they otherwise would have been. As for the provision of sanitation in the towns and of hospitals for the sick, these benefits must, if we are to judge by the example of other Asiatic nations, be ascribed almost wholly to Western influence.

Mixed Material Benefits.—I pass to a consideration of the more questionable benefits that have resulted from Western contacts. These are, broadly speaking, the characteristic products of Western industrialism. India, both for good and evil, has been brought within the orbit of the world industrial system and now traffics largely in commodities, producing, exporting and importing after the manner of the European countries. She has not yet, however, attained to a European pitch of efficiency in the manufacture of the instruments of human slaughter. This may come later.

Indian industrial development has, during the last hundred years, proceeded to such purpose that India has now been accorded representation on the Council of the International Labour Office at Geneva as one of the eight chief industrial countries of the world. The value of Indian external trade was in 1930 surpassed by that of only five countries, namely, the United States, the United Kingdom, Germany, France, and Canada. It has been computed that India's sea-borne exports during the time of Akbar, the great Mogul Emperor, could have been adequately accommodated in the hold of a moderate-sized modern cargo ship of 5000 tons gross, sailing once a month. But in 1930 ships exceeding 8,000,000 gross tonnage cleared with cargo from Indian ports. In 1929 the value of Indian imports of motor vehicles alone exceeded her total value of imports of all merchandise (except gold and silver) a century before. India has at all times been an importer of precious metals. What these imports amounted to in Akbar's time we do not know ; in 1834, however, their value was £1,750,000; in 1929 it had risen to £19,000,000. These are sample figures which may be taken as typical of the general increase in trade.

Textile Industry.—Perhaps the most striking example of the growth of Indian industrialisation is afforded by the development of the textile industries. The first cotton mill was started in Bombay in 1851. In 1935 there were 365 cotton mills in India, working 9,613,174 spindles and 194,998 looms, and the average number of mill hands employed daily amounted to 385,000. The value of the cotton goods spun throughout India as a whole—that is to say, in the Indian States as well as in British India—amounted in 1934 to £921,000,000 and of woven goods to £645,500,000. Jute mills, which numbered only 21 in 1879, had by 1932 increased to 103, employing on an average 277,000 persons daily. The textile and jute industries have been largely concentrated in two towns, cotton in Bombay and jute in Calcutta. During the last two or three years, however, Indian industries have spread and ramified in many directions. Factories have been erected at a considerable distance from the coast, gold mines have been sunk and cement works constructed in all parts of India. A crop of new industries has sprung up since the war. There are factories for the manufacture of iron and steel, match factories and paper mills, while the use of electricity is spreading everywhere. India, in fact, is in the throes of an industrial revolution, with the result that hundreds of thousands of men and women who previously made their living by agriculture in the country are now working in factories in the towns.

Effects of India's Industrial Revolution.—History shows that the immediate consequences of an industrial revolution for the vast majority of those affected by it have been almost uniformly bad. At this point, then, we turn to the debit side of India's account with the West. Unfortunately it is heavy. Let us, first, take a glance at some population figures. There are in India some 350,000,000 people. At the Census of 1921 some 73 per cent. of these were engaged in agriculture, 10.5 per cent. in industry and 7 per cent. in trade and transport. Of the 33,000,000 returned as *industrial* workers, 15,500,000 were described as actual workers and 17,500,000 as their dependents. The 1931 Census showed a considerable diminution in the number of workers employed in agriculture (from 73 to 67 per cent.) and a corresponding increase in the numbers of industrial workers. We may conclude, then, that within the last seventy years, some 30,000,000 persons who had previously worked on the land have, as a result of contact with the West, been drafted into the towns. Under what conditions? So far as housing and sanitation are concerned, under the very worst. There is a great scarcity of suitable workers' dwellings. In many Indian cities the housing accommodation of the workers is described as appalling, while the sanitary arrangements are elementary in the extreme. The notorious unhealthiness and inefficiency of Indian factory workers are ascribed by responsible observers very largely to the conditions in which they are forced to live and work. So scanty is the accommodation in the towns that many of those who come to them are compelled to leave their wives and families in the country and to live bachelor lives in tenements. There is, thus, a marked disparity between the numbers of the sexes in the working-class quarters of the big towns, a disparity which extends also to the clerks and other black-coated workers. The disparity has produced its inevitable crop of social and sexual problems. It is difficult to believe that these results of contact with the West have increased the happiness of Indians. So much for the conditions of poor Indians in the towns! What of the lot of those who still live in the country?

The Plight of the Agricultural Worker.—Indians working on the land are, broadly speaking, either tenant farmers or peasant holders. In the case of the tenant farmer, the landlord pays to the State either a variable rent periodically assessed or else a permanent rent fixed in perpetuity, and the tenant pays to the landlord whatever rent the latter can exact and the former afford. The cultivator of the peasant holding pays direct to the State a charge which in most cases is permanently fixed. In return for this he receives from the State protection from violence; his security, in fact, is guaranteed. But that is all, for, his security once ensured, the responsibility of the Indian Government towards him ends. The Government does not, for example, hold itself responsible for finding a market for his agricultural produce, nor does it seek to control the fluctuation of prices, nor has it succeeded in evolving any scheme for financing the peasant holder to enable him to carry on during periods of depression. The result is that the Indian peasant, ignorant of the larger movements of finance and trade which in the twentieth century determine the world level of prices, finds himself in times of depression unable to market his produce at a price which will yield even the meagrest of livelihoods. Every class of Indian agricultural producer is, at the present time, affected by this disastrous absence of a screen between him and the unrestricted incidence of the effects of world depression. The industrial countries which take their raw materials from India do not pay any attention either to the conditions of the needs of Indian producers, with the result that the Indian peasant, caught in the toils of the modern industrial system, finds himself increasingly driven to resort to moneylenders in order to pay his rent and keep his land under cultivation. The exorbitant interest which moneylenders charge for their loans eats into his capital, and only too often he is forced to give up his holding and go to swell the crowds of factory workers in the towns.

In all these respects contact with the West has definitely worsened the condition of the ordinary Indian peasant. It has raised the cost of his living without increasing that of the proceeds of his labour, and has made it increasingly difficult for him to wring a livelihood from the soil. Nor is this all. There is to-day in India a definite shortage of agricultural employment, and those who have no land of their own are driven into the towns by their inability to find employment in the villages. The rates of wages prevailing in the towns are, as we shall see in a moment, exceedingly low. But those who succeed in getting paid work in the country are paid even lower rates than their fellow-workers in the town. To take a sample case, the average wage of agricultural labourers in rural areas in the Punjab varied in 1927 between 6d. and 1s. 1d. a day.

Thus the effect of contact with the West upon the condition of the average Indian agricultural worker has on the whole been harmful. It is harder than it used to be for a man to make a living in the country, and as a result the Indian goes increasingly to seek his fortune in the towns. What sort of fortune does he find?

Industrial Wages.—The industrial wage level of India is extremely low, as low as it was in England in the early days of the Industrial Revolution. An inquiry conducted by the Bombay Labour Office in 1930 revealed that the average daily earnings of a Bombay mill-hand were Rs. 1/3 (1 Rupee 3 Annas, roughly equivalent to 1s. 9d.) for men and — 9/9 (9 Annas 9 Pies, roughly equivalent to 10d.) for women. In Ahmedabad they were Rs. 1/5 (1s. 11d.) a day for men and — 11/9 (1s.) a day for women. These again are sample figures. From them it may be safely deduced that the people of India are desperately poor: poverty is, indeed, the most outstanding and pervasive characteristic of the lot of the average Indian. The price which human beings are commonly required to pay for poverty is suffering and disease. Nor have Indians escaped the common payment. The diseases of India are the typical diseases of malnutrition and bad sanitation, rickets and consumption, typhoid and malaria. Because of the incidence of these diseases the lives of most Indians are, in Hobbes's famous phrase, " poor, nasty, brutish and short ". In England and Wales, where the birth-rate is 14.4 per thousand of the population, sixty-four out of every thousand babies born die in the first year of life. In British India, where it is 34.3 per thousand, the number dying in the first year of life is in the neighbourhood of 260. Precise figures for the country as a whole are not available but we may cite one or two typical cases. In Lucknow, of every thousand babies born in 1930, 329 died. In Calcutta in the same year, the death rate per thousand infants was 268, in Madras 246, in Delhi 199, in Bombay 298, and so on. The causes of this enormous mortality were the low vitality of the parents, the primitive and insanitary methods of the midwives, the debility and malformation of the babies themselves, and the appalling overcrowding of the totally inadequate tenements. In India in a normal season the foodstuffs of every kind available for daily human consumption average only 1.2 lbs. per head, or about 380 lbs. a year. It is estimated that the average Englishman's consumption of food and drink in the course of one year is almost exactly one ton. Interesting figures of foodstuffs consumed on an average annually by Englishmen are 34lbs. of pig, 64 lbs. of beef and 32 lbs. of mutton. It is, of course, possible that Englishmen require more nourishment to keep themselves alive than Indians; but scarcely, one would have thought, so much more. Thus, in spite of her contact with the West, the economic condition of India as reflected in the lives of the great mass of Indians remains extremely bad.

Indians are said to despise the body, and it is no doubt true that India has always stood for a spiritual conception of life. As, however, we contemplate the sample figures, of overcrowding and poverty and suffering and untimely death, given above, the conclusion is forced upon us that unless the standard of living of most Indians can be substantially raised, they will remain, as they are to-day, too crippled by hunger and disease to have time and energy to spare for the arts and graces of civilisation in this world, and too ridden by desire, the desire for the wherewithal to eat, to drink, to be warm and at rest, to enjoy any but the slenderest chance of that escape from craving which Indian sages prescribes to them as the passport to the next.

The Brahmo-Samaj Movement (A.D. 1830).—Let us now turn to the cultural side of India's account with the West. India has to thank the West for two things, for a partial liberation from the bonds of a decaying tradition of life and thought, and for the specifically Western conception that rights entail duties. I will say a word about each of these in turn.

It was inevitable that the impact of the West in the eighteenth century should have had considerable cultural and intellectual repercussions. Yet these took a surprisingly long time to show themselves on the surface of Indian life. When they at last did so, it was in the form of a movement for purification and reform. This movement, known as the Brahmo-Samaj, was founded by a distinguished Bengali, Rajah Ram Mohan Roy. The Brahmo-Samaj movement had two objects, the first of which was to bring India culturally, socially and intellectually into line with modern Europe. The method proposed for achieving this end was the formation of an intellectual *élite* which, working from the centre outwards, would ultimately permeate the whole mass, thus bringing every peasant and every factory worker into touch with modern ideas. The ideas which it was more particularly hoped to spread by this means were those engendered by modern science.

The second object of the Brahmo-Samaj was to encourage the study of ancient Indian literature and culture. This element of revival and return may seem to accord ill with the drive towards modernisation. If, however, we identify the aim of the Brahmo-Samaj with the attempt to make available for every Indian man and woman the best of the culture of two civilisations, the modern civilisation of the West and the traditional civilisation of India, the emphasis upon the value of the Indian literature and thought of the past becomes intelligible enough. This in the nineteenth century had become a close preserve of pedants, and, encumbered with commentaries and commentaries upon commentaries, had almost disappeared under the weight of learning which had descended upon it. To strip away this husk of later accretions from what was best in the poetry and drama and philosophy of India was one of the objects of the new movement. The Brahmo-Samaj also gave an impetus to the growth and development of the Indian vernaculars. This was particularly needed, and its effects have been particularly salutary in the case of Bengali, which, in respect of its adaptability and elasticity of expression, beauty and variety of construction, and ability to convey abstract thought, is held to be the equal of any modern European language. Rabindranath Tagore, the modern Indian poet, has written largely in Bengali, although he himself was born in a Brahmin family and was reared in the strict classical traditions. To-day, after many years of activity along the lines indicated, the Brahmo-Samaj movement has gradually become merged in the modern Indian educational and social system, but its contribution to the liberalisation of Indian ideas and institutions over the last fifty years has been one of the very greatest importance.

Effects of English Writers and English Policy Contrasted.—But the emancipating influence of the West has not been confined to the freeing of Indian thought from the bondage of old traditions. In India as elsewhere the influence of the West has acted like a yeast, setting up a process of fermentation whose limits none as yet can guess. Up to the present this process has chiefly found expression in the political sphere, where it has engendered a passionate affirmation of Indian nationalism and an equally passionate desire for freedom from British domination. This is not the place for an examination of this controversial issue. There are, however, two observations which may appropriately be made, since they will serve to indicate two of the most important of the contributions which the West has made to the development of Indian thought.

The first relates to the conception of self-government. During the last fifty years young Indians have read, and read deeply, the works of English political thinkers. Such men as J. S. Mill and Carlyle in the nineteenth century, H. G. Wells and Bertrand Russell in the twentieth, make a special appeal to a country imbued with a passionate desire for political freedom, and clamouring for the right of national self-expression. I have often heard Indian students complain that England has made them free of her political literature, while strictly forbidding them to practise what her writers preach; that she encourages them to be liberal, even revolutionary, in thought, provided that they are conservative and docile in practice. Ramsay MacDonald, when a young man still interested in reform, wrote a book in the Home University Library on Socialism, whose importation into India was by an irony of fate forbidden during the period when its author was Prime Minister. The case is typical of the difference between the attitudes which the English adopt when they are respectively writing for mankind and governing it; it also serves to explain the different sentiments which their literature and their politics respectively inspire among the governed. For it cannot be doubted that the English writers and thinkers have played a large part in generating in the Indian consciousness that demand for national self-government which English statesmen are doing their not very successful best to moderate.

Rights Entail Duties.—In the second place, English writers have insisted that rights entail duties. If you have power and place in a country, you are required, they have taught, to use your power and hold your place in trust for the country's good. If, in other words, one is born with rights and privileges, one has a duty to those who are less fortunate. These doctrines of the great socialist thinkers and revolutionaries of the West have begun to penetrate the modern Indian consciousness, and the independence movement is inspired as much by the demand of Indian idealists for the right to try their hands at administering the continent of India for the benefit of its teeming inhabitants, as by the promptings of a militant nationalism or the ambition of a privileged class.) I do not wish to suggest that the granting of self-government to India would necessarily have the effect of improving the condition of its inhabitants. The evidence seems, indeed, to be in favour of the view that its immediate results might even be harmful. I am merely pointing out that the desire for the betterment of the Indian masses is one of the many driving forces behind the present political demand. That this desire, with the acceptance of the political and social obligations which it implies, is a comparatively new thing in Indian consciousness, and that it springs at least in part from the conceptions which have come from the West is, I think, undeniable. For hundreds of years Indians did in fact rule India, but it cannot be said that during that time the condition of the people was noticeably better than it is under European rule. Indeed, it does not seem to have occurred to the average Indian ruler of the past that it was his duty to improve the condition of his subjects. The fact that the duty is now recognised in theory does not, of course, mean that the amelioration which the recognition implies would, in a self-governing India, take place in practice. But the recognition exists and is, I suggest, in large part due to Western influence.

India and the Non-Resistance Movement.—Other aspects of the movement for independence are less admirable. The traditional Indian political virtues are, as I have had occasion to point out in earlier chapters, those of tolerance and non-interference. A live-and-let-live attitude to one's neighbour has always been characteristic of Indian life. At the same time Buddhism has inculcated the duty of non-violence and a stoical resignation to what fate may send. The Indians of to-day are the natural inheritors of these virtues and are instinctively imbued with these ideals. Their instinctive form of political protest is, therefore, that of non-resistance. When this is borne in mind, Gandhi's movement is seen in its proper perspective as the supreme example of the characteristically Indian form of protestant action in the political sphere. The movement has fired the enthusiasm of Indians and won the admiration of the world. Nevertheless, it is difficult to resist the conclusion that, so far at least as the present and the immediate future are concerned, it has been a failure.

Militant Nationalism.—Impressed by the impotence of the methods enjoined by tradition to combat what they conceive to be oppression and injustice, contemporary Indians are becoming increasingly imbued with the necessity of meeting the West with its own weapons. Now the nation or individual that is to use with success the weapons of the West must adopt also some part of the aggressive psychology of the West. It is, perhaps, inevitable that peoples struggling against what they regard as foreign domination should develop a consciousness which finds expression in an inflamed and militant nationalism. It is none the less regrettable; regrettable and dangerous.

Let us suppose for a moment that the kind of policy which I briefly indicated at the close of the last Chapter[1] were to be adopted by the British Government, which consented to confer upon India the same status and the same freedom as that which is enjoyed by the self-governing Dominions. With what ideals would the use of this new-won freedom be inspired? It is difficult, when talking to young Indian students to-day, to avoid the conclusion that many would like to follow the example of Japan, and, adopting from the West the ideals of military power and efficiency in slaughter by means of which the West has conquered or exploited the East, to revenge themselves upon their exploiters by imitating the very methods which their ancestors have most deplored in the past and which men of enlightenment all over the world deplore no less in the present. India, in fact, is in danger of becoming a national goddess after the Western model, complete with an historical destiny, a sacred mission, a right of expansion, and all the rest of the paraphernalia with which Western nations are, at the moment, in the habit of justifying themselves for endangering the peace of the world, whenever they wish to impose their will upon weaker neighbours. Whether Indians could, in the light of their history and racial temperament, successfully imitate the restless self-assertion of the West is open to doubt. Restlessness and self-assertiveness are the characteristics of young peoples, and the Indians are a very ancient people. What is disquieting is that in increasing numbers they should wish to

[1] See Chapter V, pp. 125, 126.

try. To win independence is a laudable ambition, and, if independence is not to be conceded to the demands of justice, it is at least arguable that it may be right to seek to obtain it by force. The responsibility of the British is to see that they do not, by refusing the former, thrust upon Indians the necessity of having recourse to the latter; the responsibility of the Indians that they do not develop as a by-product of their struggle for independence an admiration for aggression for its own sake, and exploit the nation's longing for freedom in order to enthrone in freedom's stead a new goddess, the goddess "India," sister of "Britannia" and "La France" and "The Fatherland", upon whose altar the lives and happiness of citizens will be sacrificed to gratify Her demands for national glory and prestige. If Indians wish to learn from the political and social achievements of the West, there are many models for them to imitate, many admirable qualities for them to acquire; public spirit, for example, and zeal for reform and the subordination of the self to the public good. Let them not also adopt the false ideals to the service of which these good qualities have only too often been harnessed.

These observations have an application beyond the sphere of immediate politics.

Indian and Western Cultural Ideals.—There is at the moment a danger that Indians may adopt the less desirable not only of the political but of the cultural ideals of the West, and imitate the vulgarity as well as the aggressiveness of twentieth century

Europe. The disabling weakness of modern Western civilisation is the disparity between mechanical power and social wisdom. Science has given Western man powers fit for the gods and he brings to their use the mentality of schoolboys. Exceeding all his ancestors in his possession of the means to the good life, the contemporary Westerner exceeds them also in his ignorance of how the good life should be lived. The nineteenth century talked of progress because, by the aid of a few scientific inventions, it succeeded in establishing a society which mistook comfort for civilisation. The twentieth has substituted speed for comfort, and embraces as its distinctive ideal the rapid alteration of the position in space of pieces of matter. For the rest it identifies civilisation with the multiplicity of gadgets, lives a "press-the-button" existence, mistakes cleanliness for culture, and conceives heaven as a place in which, surrounded with buttons and switches, man can delegate to machines the business of living. These are not, it is obvious, the only possible ideals of civilised men. They have not, for example, attracted the Chinese. Let the reader savour the humorous contempt of the following quotation from the Chinese writer, Lin Yutang's book, *My Country and My People*. "Since the invention of the flush toilet and the vacuum carpet cleaner, the modern man seems to judge a man's moral standard by his cleanliness, and thinks a dog more highly civilised for having a weekly bath and a winter wrap around his belly." Thus with a phrase are valued and dismissed the characteristic ideals of the West.

The Problem for Indian Civilisation.—The cultural problem which confronts Indian civilisation may be stated very simply. It is the problem of learning to use, even to invent, the comforts and amenities of life without being enslaved by them, to take from the West its gadgets without its pathetic inability to see beyond them.

The effects produced by the impact of modern Western civilisation upon the peoples of Asia have been very various. The Japanese, for example, have incorporated many of the vices of Western civilisation—its aggressiveness, its nationalism, its belief that it is virtuous to make oneself the master of portions of the territory of other nations in fulfilment of "national destinies" and "civilising missions", its efficiency in slaughter, its willingness to sacrifice the graces and pleasures of cultivated living to the accumulation of the instruments of destruction—and few of its virtues. The Chinese, recognising the danger, have decided to learn from Europe without imitating her. But what in the West is thought worthy to be learned and what should be rejected as undesirable, depends very largely upon the existing ideals of the prospective pupil. Take, for example, the question of material needs. Western civilisation is distinguished from its predecessors by two outstanding characteristics—first, the enormous accumulations which Westerners have made of material objects, and, secondly, the frequency and the rapidity with which they wish and are able to alter the positions of these objects in space. In other words, the West is remarkable for the production of quantities of consumable goods and for speed of movement. Of the quantities of goods the Chinese are apt to be contemptuous. As Lin Yutang, in the book to which I have already referred, points out, " the Westerners have a greater capacity for getting and making more things and a lesser ability to enjoy them, while the Chinese have a greater determination and capacity to enjoy the few things they have." For this reason, it is unlikely that the Chinese will ever follow the West in identifying the good life with the possession of large quantities of objects. Nor have they shown any disposition to value as an end in itself the rapid displacement of their bodies in space. Again, the Chinese do not share the admiration of the West for machines. To quote Lin Yutang again, "a machine is always inhuman, and the Chinese hate anything inhuman."

The Indians have, it would seem, historically shared the Chinese distrust of machines. At any rate they have shown no disposition to invent them and but little aptitude in acquiring from the West the art of their management. But, while resembling the Chinese in their incapacity for admiring speed and worshipping mechanisms, they differ from them in their attitude to material objects. For Indians have not shared the Chinese " determination and capacity to enjoy the few things they have ". In this respect, their scales of values seem to have been even more remote from the West than those of the Chinese. The Chinese, at least, wish to make the most of this world, and regard the perfection of the arts of human intercourse and civility as the highest end of man. "The true end, the Chinese have decided, in a singularly clear manner, lies in the enjoyment of a simple life, especially the family life, and in harmonious social relationships." Such is Mr. Lin Yutang's summary of Chinese philosophy.

Now the philosophy of India, as we saw in Chapter II, issues in a very different conclusion. It is not to the perfection of intercourse with other human beings in this life, but to the perfection of the human soul through a multitude of lives that Hindu philosophy looks for the true end of man. To the perfection of the human soul so conceived, the possession of material objects is not only not an aid; it is a definite encumbrance, riveting the soul's attention upon the world of matter, engendering in it a craving for material things and so delaying its wished emancipation from the chain of births and rebirths. It is to be expected, therefore, that Indians should find in the ideals and achievements of the West even less ground for admiration than the Chinese. A well-known contemporary Indian philosopher, Professor Radakrishnan, quotes with effect a remark addressed by a Russian peasant to Maxim Gorki: "You can fly in the air like birds and swim in the sea like fishes, but how to live upon the earth you do not yet know." Whether the stricture upon Western civilisation implied in this comment is in all respects just, it is not my purpose here to enquire. I quote it, because it crystallises and expresses with aptness and exactitude the traditional Indian attitude to the vaunted material achievements of the West.

The Need of India.—In spite, however, of the dangers at which I have glanced, it is difficult to resist the conclusion that India would benefit from a prudent and discriminating acceptance of the goods of the West. Let me cite an example. In India many children are blind. Their blindness is due to a disease, *ophthalmia neonatorum*, which can be prevented by washing the eyes of new-born babies with silver nitrate. Many images and temples in India are encrusted with great quantities of silver. If some of this silver were stripped away and dissolved in nitric acid, and the resultant silver nitrate were applied to the cure of blindness, many Indian children who to-day are blind would be able to see. It is unlikely that many Indians have critically taken note of this blindness of Indian children. If, however, it were brought to their notice, and the remedy suggested, they would almost certainly resist the stripping away of the silver required for the remedial nitrate, on the ground that it would be sacrilege.

The point has a symbolic significance. What it symbolises is the indifference which Indians still maintain to the goods of this world, because of the pre-occupation of their philosophy and religion with the reality of another. It is difficult not to deplore the results of this indifference. What at the moment seems to be required is a judicious blend of Western materialism and Indian spirituality. The prospects of Indian civilisation depend, in other words, upon the ability of Indians to take over and to adapt the material goods of Western civilisation without falling a victim to the characteristic Western inability to see beyond them, to use them, in other words, as means to ends beyond themselves, instead of mistaking them for ends in themselves. It will be interesting to see whether this feat proves to be possible.